HEINEMANN

SHAKESPEARE

The Winter's Tale

edited by Andrew Worrall

with additional notes and activities by
Rick Lee, Rob Chambers and Ken Elliott

Series Editor: John Seely

Heinemann Educational Publishers
Halley Court, Jordan Hill, Oxford OX2 8EJ
a division of Reed Educational and Professional Publishing Ltd

MELBOURNE AUCKLAND
FLORENCE PRAGUE MADRID ATHENS
SINGAPORE TOKYO SÃO PAULO
CHICAGO PORTSMOUTH NH MEXICO
IBADAN GABORONE JOHANNESBURG
KAMPALA NAIROBI

First published in the *Heinemann Advanced Shakespeare* series 1996

2000 99 98 97 96
10 9 8 7 6 5 4 3 2 1

A catalogue record for this book is available from the British Library
on request.
ISBN 0435 19302 3

Cover design by Miller Craig and Cocking
Cover photograph from Donald Cooper

Page make-up by Sharon Rudd

Produced by Celia Floyd, Basingstoke

Printed and bound in the United Kingdom by Clays Ltd, St Ives plc

Contents

How to use this book

This edition of *The Winter's Tale* has been prepared to
provide students with several different kinds of information
and guidance.

The introduction

Before the text of the play there is:
- the story of the play
- background information about where Shakespeare got
  the story from and how he adapted it for his purposes
- a brief explanation of Shakespeare's texts.

The text and commentary

On each right-hand page you will find the text of the play.
On the facing left-hand pages there are three types of
support material:
- a summary of the action
- detailed explanations of difficult words, phrases and
  longer sections of text
- suggestions of points you might find it useful to think
  about as you read the play.

End-of-act activities

After each act there is a set of activities. These can be
tackled as you read the play. Many students, however, may
want to leave these until they undertake a second reading.
They consist of the following.

Keeping track: straightforward questions directing your
attention to the action of the act.

Characters: questions that help to guide your study of the
changing perspectives of the characters.

Themes: pointers to the ideas behind Shakespeare's thinking
as he constructed the play.

Drama: practical drama activities to help you focus on key
characters, relationships and situations.

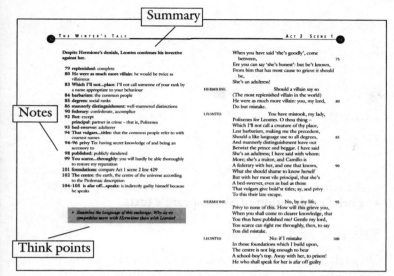

Summary

Notes

Think points

Despite Hermione's denials, Leontes continues his invective against her.

79 **replenished**: complete
80 **He were as much more villain**: he would be twice as villainous
83 **Which I'll not...place**: I'll not call someone of your rank by a name appropriate to your behaviour
84 **barbarism**: the common people
85 **degrees**: social ranks
86 **mannerly distinguishment**: well-mannered distinctions
90 **federary**: confederate, accomplice
92 **But**: except
    principal: partner in crime – that is, Polixenes
93 **bed-swerver**: adulterer
94 **That vulgars...titles**: that the common people refer to with coarsest names
94–96 **privy To**: having secret knowledge of and being an accessory to
98 **published**: publicly slandered
99 **You scarce...throughly**: you will hardly be able thoroughly to restore my reputation
101 **foundations**: compare Act 1 scene 2 line 429
102 **The centre**: the earth, the centre of the universe according to the Ptolemaic description
104–105 **is afar off...speaks**: is indirectly guilty himself because he speaks

• *Examine the language of this exchange. Why do my sympathies more with Hermione than with Leontes?*

> When you have said 'she's goodly', come between,   75
> Ere you can say 'she's honest': but be't known,
> From him that has most cause to grieve it should be,
> She's an adultress!
>
> HERMIONE   Should a villain say so
> (The most replenished villain in the world)
> He were as much more villain: you, my lord,   80
> Do but mistake.
>
> LEONTES   You have mistook, my lady,
> Polixenes for Leontes. O thou thing –
> Which I'll not call a creature of thy place,
> Lest barbarism, making me the precedent,
> Should a like language use to all degrees,   85
> And mannerly distinguishment leave out
> Betwixt the prince and beggar. I have said
> She's an adultress; I have said with whom:
> More; she's a traitor, and Camillo is
> A federary with her, and one that knows,   90
> What she should shame to know herself
> But with her most vile principal, that she's
> A bed-swerver, even as bad as those
> That vulgars give bold'st titles; ay, and privy
> To this their late escape.
>
> HERMIONE   No, by my life,   95
> Privy to none of this. How will this grieve you,
> When you shall come to clearer knowledge, that
> You thus have published me? Gentle my lord,
> You scarce can right me throughly, then, to say
> You did mistake.
>
> LEONTES   No: if I mistake   100
> In those foundations which I build upon,
> The centre is not big enough to bear
> A school-boy's top. Away with her, to prison!
> He who shall speak for her is afar off guilty

Close study: work on the text of selected extracts from the play, designed to help you tackle Shakespeare's language in detail.

Key scene: a focus on an important scene in the act. This is intended to help you combine an understanding of the characters and broader themes of the play with the ability to comment on the text in detail.

Writing: progressive activities throughout the book help you to develop essay writing skills.

Explorations

At the end of the book a number of guidelines are provided to draw together your thoughts and insights on the play:

- how to approach thinking about the whole play
- work on character
- work on the themes and issues
- notes on the language of the play, and on the play as a theatrical experience
- guidance on how to tackle practical drama activities
- advice on preparing for an examination
- advice on essay writing, and practical essay questions
- glossary of technical terms.

The story of the play

Act 1

Polixenes, King of Bohemia, is the guest of his old friend **Leontes**, King of Sicilia. Polixenes has been in Sicilia for nine months and is keen, despite his lavish treatment and the persuasion of Leontes, to return to his kingdom and to his young son. But when **Hermione**, Leontes' queen, speaks to Polixenes he agrees to stay longer.

Suddenly, Leontes is suspicious of the relationship between Hermione and Polixenes. He begins to see signs of adultery in her playful behaviour towards their guest. His jealous anger is all the greater because he looks upon Polixenes as his brother. He begins to suspect that Hermione, who is pregnant, is about to bear Polixenes' child.

Leontes discloses his suspicions to his faithful courtier, **Camillo**, who finds the story incredible. When Leontes commands him to murder the King of Bohemia, Camillo reveals the plot to Polixenes and escapes from Sicilia with him.

Act 2

Leontes has Hermione arrested. She is separated from **Mamillius**, her young son, who immediately becomes ill. None of Leontes' courtiers believes Hermione is guilty but the king tells them that he will demonstrate the truth of his suspicions by sending to the Oracle of Apollo for spiritual counsel.

Hermione gives birth in prison to a daughter. A noblewoman, **Paulina**, takes the baby to court in an attempt to make Leontes see reason but he rejects it and commands **Antigonus**, Paulina's husband, to destroy the baby by taking it to some foreign country and there exposing it to the elements.

Two courtiers, **Cleomenes** and **Dion**, return with a sealed message from Apollo's Oracle. Leontes puts Hermione on trial for treason and adultery. She defends herself nobly but nothing she can say will change Leontes' mind. Finally she calls upon the judgement of Apollo. The message from the Oracle is opened and read. It reveals that Hermione, Polixenes and

Camillo are innocent. Leontes is proclaimed a jealous tyrant and told that he will live without an heir if his daughter is not found. Leontes dismisses the Oracle as a fraud but when a servant enters to announce that Mamillius has died, Leontes repents his rashness. Hermione collapses and is carried out by Paulina. Paulina returns to tell Leontes that his queen has died. Having destroyed his family, Leontes is filled with shame and remorse.

Act 3

Antigonus has arrived on the shores of Bohemia where he intends to leave the baby. He has been told to go there by Hermione whom he has seen in a dream. She has instructed him to call the child **Perdita**. He lays Perdita on the ground with a box of gold, Hermione's shawl and papers detailing who she is. A wild storm breaks, his ship is sunk and a bear pursues Antigonus, kills and eats him.

An **Old Shepherd** enters and finds Perdita. He is joined by his son, the **Clown**, who has seen the shipwreck (in which all the mariners have died) and the death of Antigonus. They bury the remains of Antigonus and, deciding that Perdita must have been left by the fairies (since they cannot read Antigonus' documents), agree to keep her and the gold but not to reveal the events they have witnessed.

Act 4

Sixteen years have passed and the events are summarized by **Time**, a Chorus. Perdita has grown up believing that she is the daughter of the Old Shepherd.

Polixenes is concerned that his son and heir, **Florizel**, is often away from the court, attracted by the daughter of an unaccountably rich shepherd. Determined to stop his son's affair, Polixenes decides that he and Camillo (who is now his trusted adviser) should go in disguise to question the shepherd.

Autolycus, a clever rogue who had once been Florizel's servant, meets the foolish Clown. He tricks the Clown of his money and learns that the Old Shepherd is organizing a sheep-shearing feast. This will allow Autolycus further scope for stealing and cheating.

At the feast Florizel, disguised as a shepherd, woos Perdita. Polixenes and Camillo arrive in disguise and are treated as honoured guests. Polixenes is surprised by the beauty and wit of Perdita but remains determined to see his son separated from her. There is dancing and Autolycus, now disguised as a peddler, arrives with songs and wares to sell. Amidst the festivities Florizel announces his intention to marry Perdita.

Polixenes intervenes, reveals himself and threatens to disinherit his son while having the Old Shepherd and Perdita executed. He leaves, commanding Florizel to return to court, but the prince repeats his vows to Perdita and proposes to elope with her. Camillo reveals himself and offers to help the young couple. He suggests that they should set sail for Sicilia and pretend to be ambassadors to Leontes who have come to heal the sixteen-year rift between the two kings. Camillo sees this as providing himself with a pretext for returning to Sicilia, which he would like to revisit before he dies.

The prince accepts Camillo's advice and disguises himself once more by exchanging clothes with Autolycus (who has robbed and cheated the revellers). While Florizel and Perdita set off for the prince's ship, Camillo goes to reveal their plan to Polixenes in order to persuade him to follow his son to Sicilia.

Autolycus, now wearing the clothes previously worn by Florizel, meets the Old Shepherd and the Clown who, terrified of the king's sentence, have decided to go to Polixenes with the evidence of Perdita's identity. They don't know what the writing says but they know it will prove that she is not their flesh and blood and that therefore they are not responsible for her. Autolycus, true to his roguish credentials, deceives the rustics into believing that he is an influential courtier. They agree to accompany him to the king but he decides to take them to Florizel's ship in the hope of further profit.

Act 5

In Sicilia the penitent Leontes has not ceased to mourn his lost wife and children. Despite encouragement from some courtiers he refuses to re-marry. Paulina supports him and extracts from him an oath not to marry unless she herself selects a bride identical to Hermione.

Unexpectedly Florizel and Perdita arrive, she pretending to be the daughter of the King of Libya. Leontes welcomes them warmly, being especially struck by the beauty of Perdita and her likeness to Hermione, but is interrupted by the arrival of Polixenes in hot pursuit. Leontes goes to meet him, promising to speak to him on Florizel's behalf.

Autolycus enters and, in conversation with three gentlemen discovers that, off stage, the Old Shepherd and Clown have finally been able to tell their story and all has been revealed concerning Perdita's birth. There can be no impediment to Florizel and Perdita's marriage and the Old Shepherd and the Clown have been reborn as Gentlemen. The kings and their courtiers rejoice because, now that Perdita has been found, the Oracle is fulfilled and Leontes has an heir. All go to view a statue of Hermione which Paulina has commissioned.

The final scene takes place in Paulina's house. She reveals Hermione's statue which is astonishingly lifelike. Leontes is overcome with its realism and believes he sees it breathe. Paulina offers to make it speak and move providing that none will believe she is guilty of witchcraft. Accompanied by the healing harmony of music Hermione moves, kisses Leontes and blesses Perdita, the daughter she last saw as a baby. She reveals that, hearing that the Oracle gave some hope of Perdita's survival, she has lived in secret, protected by Paulina. Thus all are reunited, and even Paulina gets a new husband, Camillo. Time, which tests all people, is also shown to be a supreme healer.

Background

When the play begins we are introduced to characters who seem to be from the world of fairy tales, and we don't find too much difficulty in accepting them. We are used to such fantasy worlds and they follow a certain kind of logic. But *The Winter's Tale* quickly upsets our expectations. Leontes' extraordinary jealousy and madness followed by a rapid and abrupt mixture of tragic and comic incident can be difficult for a modern audience to respond to.

In some respects Shakespeare's original audience had an advantage over us. The playwright used one major source for his play: *Pandosto, The Triumph of Time*, a prose romance – a sort of early novel – by Robert Greene. First published in 1588 it was reprinted three times in the following nine years and adapted by other publishers, which suggests that it was a popular success and that many in Shakespeare's audience would have known the story. Shakespeare makes some striking changes to plot and characters, however. Not only does he re-name all the characters but he creates Paulina, Antigonus and Autolycus. The greatest differences are in the tone and purposes of the story. In *Pandosto* Hermione dies and Leontes commits suicide. Greene's concern was to provide a moral tale 'profitable for youth' (the subtitle to *Pandosto*). But like Greene, Shakespeare refers to conventions of storytelling which were familiar in the seventeenth century but much less so now. We look at some of these in the EXPLORATIONS section at the end of this edition (pages 245–268).

Shakespeare provides a fireside fairy story, 'an old tale still', which we need to recognize as a fantasy not too distant from modern science fiction with its own internal sense of logic and order. We'll really enjoy the experience if we are prepared to suspend our reason and allow ourselves to be carried along by the speed and variety of events.

The text of Shakespeare's plays

Shakespeare's work is generally treated with such immense respect that it may seem strange to admit that we cannot be certain exactly what he wrote. The reasons for this mystery lie in the circumstances of the theatre and publishing in the sixteenth and seventeenth centuries.

Shakespeare was a professional writer and shareholder in a company of actors, the Lord Chamberlain's Men, for whom he wrote his plays. Since copyright and performing rights did not exist before the eighteenth century, there was always the risk that if a play was successful other companies would perform it and reap the financial rewards. To avoid this problem acting companies guarded the handwritten copy of a completed work. It was the company's most valuable resource and kept by the prompter: each actor was given only his own lines and his cues.

This lack of printed texts seems strange to modern readers but, like other playwrights of his time, Shakespeare's concern was with what his plays looked and sounded like on the stage, not what they looked like on the page.

However, there was money to be made from printed plays and during his lifetime nearly half of Shakespeare's plays were printed in what are known as quartos: paperback editions of single plays. Some of these are pirated editions based on the memories of actors and audience. Others are much more accurate and may have been authorized by Shakespeare or the sharers in his company, perhaps to capitalize on a popular success which was about to go out of repertory or to forestall a pirate edition. None, however, seems to have been supervised by the playwright and all differ, often considerably, from the key text of Shakespeare's plays, the *First Folio*.

The *First Folio*, published in 1623, is a collected edition of all Shakespeare's plays (with the exception of *Pericles*). It was edited by John Hemming and Henry Condell, two shareholders in the Lord Chamberlain's Men, using 'good' quartos, prompt copies and other company papers in an effort to provide an accurate text as a fitting memorial to their partner. They did not start the editing process until after Shakespeare died and apparently based their editorial decisions on what had happened in the theatre. We cannot be certain how far the *First Folio* represents what Shakespeare's ultimate intentions might have been.

Even if Shakespeare had approved the text which went to the printer, it was the custom for writers to leave much of the detail of spelling and punctuation to the printer or to a scribe who made a fair copy from the playwright's rough drafts. The scribe and printer thus introduced their own interpretation and inaccuracies into the text. The *First Folio* was reprinted three times in the seventeenth century and each edition corrected some inaccuracies and introduced new errors.

A modern editor tries to provide a text which is easy to read and close to Shakespeare's presumed intentions. To do this the editor may modernize spelling and change punctuation, add stage directions, act and scene divisions and make important decisions about which of several readings in quarto and folio editions is most acceptable.

If you are able to compare this edition of the play with other editions you are likely to find many minor variations between them as well as occasional major differences which could change your view of a character or situation.

The text of *The Winter's Tale*

The Winter's Tale is one of Shakespeare's last plays. It was probably written during the first four months of 1611. It is known to have been performed at the Globe Theatre on 15 May 1611 and (as part of royal wedding celebrations) at Court during 1613, by which time the playwright had retired.

The Winter's Tale was first published in the *First Folio*. It is thought that the text was printed from a manuscript copied by a professional scribe, Ralph Crane. He used heavy punctuation which is not consistent with modern practice, and there are few stage directions, but he seems to have provided the printers with clear and accurate copy: there are very few occasions when the intention of the text is not clear. In this edition spelling and some punctuation have been modernized. Some stage directions have been added. Any unresolved textual problems receive comment in the notes.

THE WINTER'S TALE

CHARACTERS

The Sicilians

LEONTES, King of Sicilia
HERMIONE, his Queen
MAMILLIUS, their son
PERDITA, their daughter

CAMILLO ⎫
ANTIGONUS ⎬ four lords
CLEOMENES ⎪
DION ⎭

PAULINA, wife of Antigonus
EMILIA, a lady attending on Hermione
A Mariner
A Gaoler
A Lord
Three Gentlemen

The Bohemians

POLIXENES, King of Bohemia
FLORIZEL, his son, also known as Doricles
ARCHIDAMUS, a lord
OLD SHEPHERD, reputed father of Perdita
CLOWN, his son
AUTOLYCUS, a rogue

MOPSA ⎫
DORCAS ⎭ shepherdesses

TIME, as Chorus

Other Lords and Gentlemen, Ladies, Officers and Servants,
Shepherds and Shepherdesses, Dancers

Sicilia. Polixenes, King of Bohemia, is visiting his dear friend
Leontes, King of Sicilia. Archidamus, a Bohemian nobleman,
tells Leontes' trusted adviser Camillo that Sicilian hospitality is
far beyond anything that Bohemia can offer. The two lords
indulge in courtly banter. They reveal that Leontes expects to
repay the visit in the near future and that the two kings
grew up together.

1–3 **on the like…on foot**: in similar circumstances to me, in
the role of trusted servant to your king on his travels abroad
6 **Bohemia**: the King of Bohemia
visitation: official visit
justly: with good reason
8–9 **Wherein our…loves**: at which time our hospitality will
compare unfavourably with yours but the strength of our love
will make up for our shortcomings
10 **Beseech you –**: please…
11 **Verily…knowledge**: truly, I speak boldly because I know from
experience
14–15 **unintelligent of our insufficiency**: having no
understanding of our inability to fulfil your needs
17–18 **You pay…freely**: you overvalue our free hospitality
21 **Sicilia**: the King of Sicilia
22–24 **trained…rooted…branch**: this metaphor is the first of
many taken from nature. Camillo intends branch to mean 'bud
and bear fruit', which will prove to be ironic.
24–26 **Since their more…society**: since growing up to positions
of high rank and royal duties caused them be parted from each
other
27 **royally attorneyed**: made through appropriately high-ranking
deputies

Act one

Scene 1

Enter CAMILLO *and* ARCHIDAMUS

ARCHIDAMUS If you shall chance, Camillo, to visit Bohemia, on the like occasion whereon my services are now on foot, you shall see, as I have said, great difference betwixt our Bohemia and your Sicilia.

CAMILLO I think, this coming summer, the King of Sicilia 5 means to pay Bohemia the visitation which he justly owes him.

ARCHIDAMUS Wherein our entertainment shall shame us: we will be justified in our loves: for indeed –

CAMILLO Beseech you – 10

ARCHIDAMUS Verily I speak it in the freedom of my knowledge: we cannot with such magnificence – in so rare – I know not what to say – We will give you sleepy drinks, that your senses (unintelligent of our insufficience) may, though they cannot praise us, 15 as little accuse us.

CAMILLO You pay a great deal too dear for what's given freely.

ARCHIDAMUS Believe me, I speak as my understanding instructs me, and as mine honesty puts it to utterance. 20

CAMILLO Sicilia cannot show himself over-kind to Bohemia. They were trained together in their childhoods, and there rooted betwixt them then such an affection which cannot choose but branch now. Since their more mature dignities and royal necessities made 25 separation of their society, their encounters, though not personal, have been royally attorneyed with

Though Leontes and Polixenes have been parted for many years they have maintained a constant and affectionate relationship. Leontes' son and heir, Mamillius, is reported to be of great promise and admired by the Sicilians.

28 embassies: messages
30 vast: great empty space, normally unbridgeable
33–34 either malice or matter: reasons, either pretended or real
39 physics the subject: is like a healing medicine for the whole nation (and thus demonstrates his fitness as heir to the throne)
46–47 If the king...one: this jest also has an ironic tone

> • *What is the tone of the conversation between Camillo and Archidamus? What mood does it establish?*

Polixenes announces his intention to return home after a stay of nine months. He effusively thanks Leontes.

1 Nine changes...star: nine lunar months. The moon is a watery star since it controls the tides. It is symbolic of womanhood, and Polixenes thus makes an unconscious reference to Hermione who is visibly pregnant (see Act 2 scene 1 lines 60–61).
2 The shepherd's note: noticed by the shepherd. Polixenes, thinking of Bohemia, associates it with shepherds, thus prefiguring Act 3 scene 3 and Act 4. As a monarch he refers to himself in the plural: 'we...our'.
3 burden: load, responsibility. Polixenes puns – he has laid aside the responsibilities of kingship and the throne has not had to bear his weight.
4 Would be: ought to be
5–6 And yet...in debt: and even then we would always be in debt to you
6–9 and therefore...before it: so like a zero, which alone means nothing yet in the right place multiplies a number, my one word of thanks multiplies all that have gone before

interchange of gifts, letters, loving embassies, that
they have seemed to be together, though absent;
shook hands, as over a vast; and embraced, as it   30
were, from the ends of opposed winds. The heavens
continue their loves!

ARCHIDAMUS I think there is not in the world either malice or
matter to alter it. You have an unspeakable comfort
of your young prince Mamillius: it is a gentleman 35
of the greatest promise that ever came into my
note.

CAMILLO I very well agree with you in the hopes of him: it is
a gallant child; one that, indeed, physics the subject,
makes old hearts fresh: they that went on   40
crutches ere he was born desire yet their life to see
him a man.

ARCHIDAMUS Would they else be content to die?

CAMILLO Yes; if there were no other excuse why they should
desire to live.   45

ARCHIDAMUS If the king had no son, they would desire to live on
crutches till he had one.   [*Exeunt*

Scene 2

Enter LEONTES, HERMIONE, MAMILLIUS, POLIXENES
and CAMILLO

POLIXENES Nine changes of the watery star hath been
The shepherd's note since we have left our throne
Without a burden. Time as long again
Would be filled up, my brother, with our thanks;
And yet we should, for perpetuity,   5
Go hence in debt: and therefore, like a cipher
(Yet standing in rich place) I multiply
With one 'We thank you' many thousands moe
That go before it.

Leontes tries to persuade Polixenes to stay longer but he
resists. He is concerned about the state of his country in his
absence and that he might have over-stayed his welcome.
Leontes asks his wife, Hermione, to speak; she suggests that
Leontes should be more passionately persuasive.

9 **Stay**: suspend

11–14 **I am questioned...truly'**: I am worried about what may
  happen or develop at home in my absence; I fear such biting
  winds which would justify my fears. The wind metaphor is
  particularly appropriate since Polixenes is contemplating a sea
  voyage.

16 **Than you...to 't**: than any test you can devise for me.
  Leontes, as a king, refers to himself in the plural.

17 **One seve'night**: a week
  Very sooth: definitely

18–19 **We'll part the time...gainsaying**: let's compromise (on
  three or four days) and I won't take no for an answer

21–23 **so it should...denied it**: I would give in to you even
  now if you had real need, even if my need to deny you were
  the greater

25 **Were...to me**: would torture me even though you love me

31–32 **this satisfaction...proclaimed**: we were pleased to hear
  that news only yesterday

33 **He's beat...ward**: you destroy his best defence. The
  metaphor is taken from fencing where a ward is a defensive
  posture or parry.

- *What role is Leontes playing? How would you describe
  his mood and behaviour towards his wife and
  Polixenes?*
- *What is the evidence of Polixenes' great affection for
  Leontes?*

| LEONTES | Stay your thanks a while, |
| | And pay them when you part. |

POLIXENES   Sir, that's to-morrow. 10
I am questioned by my fears, of what may chance
Or breed upon our absence; thay may blow
No sneaping winds at home, to make us say
'This is put forth too truly'. Besides, I have stayed
To tire your royalty.

LEONTES   We are tougher, brother, 15
Than you can put us to 't.

POLIXENES   No longer stay.

LEONTES   One seve'night longer.

POLIXENES   Very sooth, to-morrow.

LEONTES   We'll part the time between 's then: and in that
I'll no gainsaying.

POLIXENES   Press me not, beseech you, so.
There is no tongue that moves, none, none i' th'
    world,   20
So soon as yours, could win me: so it should now,
Were there necessity in your request, although
'Twere needful I denied it. My affairs
Do even drag me homeward: which to hinder
Were (in your love) a whip to me; my stay, 25
To you a charge and trouble: to save both,
Farewell, our brother.

LEONTES   Tongue-tied our queen? Speak you.

HERMIONE   I had thought, sir, to have held my peace until
You had drawn oaths from him not to stay. You, sir,
Charge him too coldly. Tell him, you are sure 30
All in Bohemia's well: this satisfaction
The by-gone day proclaimed : say this to him,
He's beat from his best ward.

LEONTES   Well said, Hermione.

HERMIONE   To tell, he longs to see his son, were strong:

Hermione teases and cajoles Polixenes into agreeing to stay in Sicilia for a further week.

37 distaff: the long rod on which wool was wound prior to spinning. Hermione would beat Polixenes into going home if he failed to keep his solemn oath that he needed to see his son. The distaff is symbolic of women's work and hence of female authority.

38 your royal presence: said to Polixenes

41 gest: the time allotted for a halt or stay, especially during a royal journey

42 good deed: indeed

43–44 I love thee...lord: I don't love you a tick of the clock less than any lady loves her husband

47 limber: limp, weak; verily (truly) is not a powerful oath

48 unsphere the stars: remove the stars from their appointed place in the heavens

53 pay your fees: a prisoner in an English gaol paid a fee on his release

57 import offending: imply that I had offended against you

> • *What techniques does Hermione employ in her persuasion of Polixenes? What actions or stage business might accompany her words?*

But let him say so then, and let him go;   35
But let him swear so, and he shall not stay,
We'll thwack him hence with distaffs.
Yet of your royal presence I'll adventure
The borrow of a week. When at Bohemia
You take my lord, I'll give him my commission   40
To let him there a month behind the gest
Prefixed for's parting : yet, good deed, Leontes
I love thee not a jar o' th' clock behind
What lady she her lord. You'll stay?

POLIXENES   No madam.

HERMIONE   Nay, but you will?

POLIXENES   I may not, verily.   45

HERMIONE   Verily!
You put me off with limber vows; but I,
Though you would seek t' unsphere the stars with
        oaths,
Should yet say 'Sir, no going'. Verily,
You shall not go: a lady's Verily's   50
As potent as a lord's. Will you go yet?
Force me to keep you as a prisoner,
Not like a guest: so you shall pay your fees
When you depart, and save your thanks? How say
        you?
My prisoner? or my guest? By your dread
        'Verily',   55
One of them you shall be.

POLIXENES   Your guest then, madam:
To be your prisoner should import offending;
Which is for me less easy to commit
Than you to punish.

HERMIONE   Not your gaoler then,
But your kind hostess. Come, I'll question you   60
Of my lord's tricks, and yours, when you were
        boys.

Hermione encourages Polixenes to talk about his childhood with Leontes. Their conversation seems playful but also describes a loss of innocence.

62 lordings: little lords; the word is used mockingly

63 behind: yet to come

66 The verier wag: the more mischievous boy

68 changed: exchanged

70 The doctrine of ill-doing: original sin; the belief held by many Christians that, as a result of the disobedience of Adam and Eve, humans are fundamentally evil

72–73 And our weak...blood: and never grown up

73–75 we should have...ours: we would have been able to tell God that we were innocent even of original sin, the inheritance of everyone. Original sin is the belief traditionally held by Christians that because of the disobedience of Adam and Eve (the Fall), all humans are morally imperfect.

76 tripped: sinned. Hermione plays on the idea of a moral fall.

78 unfledged days: early childhood – literally newly hatched, lacking feathers

80 Grace to boot!: God help me! Polixenes has cast himself and Leontes in the role of Adam. He implies that their wives have betrayed them as Eve was supposed to have betrayed Adam.

86 Is he won yet?: this question implies that Leontes has not been listening to Hermione and Polixenes. The dramatic significance of this part of the scene will be affected by Leontes' actions between lines 44 and 86.

- *What images are used to describe childhood?*
- *Consider who else is on stage during this conversation and suggest what Leontes might have been doing between lines 40 and 86.*

You were pretty lordings them?

POLIXENES   We were, fair queen,
Two lads that thought there was no more behind,
But such a day to-morrow as to-day,
And to be boy eternal.

HERMIONE   Was not my lord   65
The verier wag o' th' two?

POLIXENES We were as twinned lambs that did frisk i' th' sun,
And bleat the one at th' other: what we changed
Was innocence for innocence: we knew not
The doctrine of ill-doing, nor dreamed   70
That any did. Had we pursued that life,
And our weak spirits ne'er been higher reared
With stronger blood, we should have answered heaven
Boldly 'not guilty', the imposition cleared
Hereditary ours.

HERMIONE   By this we gather   75
You have tripped since.

POLIXENES   O my most sacred lady,
Temptations have since then been born to 's: for
In those unfledged days was my wife a girl;
Your precious self had then not crossed the eyes
Of my young play-fellow.

HERMIONE   Grace to boot!   80
Of this make no conclusion, lest you say
Your queen and I are devils. Yet go on;
Th' offences we have made you do we'll answer,
If you first sinned with us, and that with us
You did continue fault, and that you slipped not   85
With any but with us.

LEONTES   Is he won yet?

HERMIONE He'll stay, my lord.

Hermione announces that Polixenes will stay and Leontes
seems to commend her persuasiveness. He compares the
effectiveness of her speech now with the earlier occasion on
which she finally consented to marry him. In an aside
Leontes reveals the extent of his unease at the relationship
between Polixenes and Hermione.

91 **I prithee**: please; I pray you

92 **tongueless**: unspoken of

94–96 **You may ride's...acre**: kindness will encourage us mu(
more than pain. A furlong measures an eighth of a mile (22
yards); an acre is 4,840 square yards. The metaphor contras(
a long journey with struggling across a small field.

99 **Grace**: God-given virtue

102 **crabbed**: difficult, perverse. Both syllables are pronounced.

104 **clap**: declare; finalize an agreement by clasping hands

106 **lo**: look

109 **far**: too far (the comparative form, spelt *farre* in the *Folio*)

110 *tremor cordis*: palpitations of the heart

111–114 **This entertainment...agent**: this hospitality may
appear open, extrovert and be justified by a warm heart,
generosity and a desire to see friendship grow; if that is the
case it is appropriate

- *What are the indications that Hermione has control in
this scene (up to line 108)? How has she achieved this?*

LEONTES	At my request he would not.

Hermione, my dearest, thou never spok'st
To better purpose.

HERMIONE   Never?

LEONTES   Never but once.

HERMIONE   What! have I twice said well? when was't before?   90
I prithee tell me: cram 's with praise, and make's
As fat as tame things: one good deed, dying
        tongueless,
Slaughters a thousand, waiting upon that.
Our praises are our wages. You may ride's
With one soft kiss a thousand furlongs ere   95
With spur we heat an acre. But to th' goal:
My last good deed was to entreat his stay:
What was my first? It has an elder sister,
Or I mistake you: O, would her name were Grace!
But once before I spoke to th' purpose? When?   100
Nay, let me have't: I long!

LEONTES   Why, that was when
Three crabbed months had soured themselves to
        death,
Ere I could make thee open thy white hand,
And clap thyself my love; then didst thou utter
'I am yours for ever.'

HERMIONE   'Tis Grace indeed.   105
Why lo you now; I have spoke to th' purpose twice:
The one, for ever earned a royal husband;
Th' other, for some while a friend.

                                        [*Giving her hand to* POLIXENES

LEONTES   [*Aside*] Too hot, too hot!
To mingle friendship far, is mingling bloods.
I have *tremor cordis* on me: my heart dances,   110
But not for joy – not joy. This entertainment
May a free face put on, derive a liberty
From heartiness, from bounty, fertile bosom,
And well become the agent: 't may, I grant:

Leontes interprets the physical closeness of Polixenes and Hermione as a sign of their adultery. He looks at his son and wonders about the boy's paternity.

115 **paddling palms and pinching fingers**: Polixenes and Hermione are playing with each other's hands as they talk

118 **The mort o' th' deer**: the horn call made by a huntsman at the death of a deer. The image suggests the death of love (with a pun on dear) and the sigh of orgasm which is commonly called 'dying' in poetry of the period.

119 **brows**: the forehead of a deceived husband (cuckold) was supposed to grow invisible horns which all but he could see

120 **I' fecks**: in faith

121 **bawcock**: fine fellow; from the French, *beau coq*
    smutched: smudged, made dirty

125 **neat**: tidy, horned cattle; the unintended pun leads to the thought of horns which again disturbs Leontes
    virginalling: as if playing the virginals, a harpsichord

126 **wanton**: both frisky and unchaste. The word is perhaps suggested by its opposition to virginal in the previous line.

128 **pash...shoots**: head and horns, like a bull

129 **full**: fully

132 **o'er-dyed blacks**: black mourning clothes which have been dyed another colour

134 **bourn 'twixt**: boundary between

136 **welkin**: sky-blue

137 **collop**: slice of meat, hence his own flesh and blood
    dam: mother – usually only used of animals

138–146 **Affection! thy...brows)**: in this passage Leontes attempts to impose logic upon his disordered emotions. The general direction of his argument may be paraphrased as:

> Passion! Your intensity stabs my heart. You make the impossible possible, inform our dreams (I don't know how), make the unreal real and communicate with nothingness. So I have no difficulty in believing that passion can centre on something that is real: it does (though I don't want it to) and I experience it, though it drives me mad and brings me cuckold's horns.

It remains unclear whether 'Affection' refers to Hermione's apparent lust or Leontes' jealousy, or whether Leontes is now incapable of making a distinction between the two.

	But to be paddling palms, and pinching fingers, 115
	As now they are, and making practised smiles
	As in a looking-glass; and then to sigh, as 'twere
	The mort o' th' deer – O, that is entertainment
	My bosom likes not, nor my brows. Mamillius,
	Art thou my boy?

MAMILLIUS   Ay, my good lord.

LEONTES   I' fecks: 120
Why that's my bawcock. What! hast smutched thy
    nose?
They say it is a copy out of mine. Come, captain,
We must be neat; not neat, but cleanly, captain:
And yet the steer, the heifer and the calf
Are all called neat. – Still virginalling   125
Upon his palm! – How now, you wanton calf!
Art thou my calf?

MAMILLIUS   Yes, if you will, my lord.

LEONTES   Thou want'st a rough pash and the shoots that I
           have
To be full like me: yet they say we are
Almost as like as eggs; women say so,   130
(That will say any thing) : but were they false
As o'er-dyed blacks, as wind, as waters; false
As dice are to be wished by one that fixes
No bourn 'twixt his and mine, yet were it true
To say this boy were like me. Come, sir page,   135
Look on me with your welkin eye: sweet villain!
Most dear'st, my collop! Can thy dam? – may't
    be? –
Affection! thy intention stabs the centre:
Thou dost make possible things not so held,
Communicat'st with dreams; – how can this
    be? –   140
With what's unreal thou coactive art,
And fellow'st nothing: then 'tis very credent
Thou may'st co-join with something; and thou

Polixenes and Hermione notice Leontes' distress but he
pretends merely to have been prompted by his observation o
Mamillius to remember his own childhood. Questioned by
Leontes, Polixenes enlarges on his affection for his son.

148 What cheer?...brother?: How are you? Are you well? The
First Folio gives this line to Leontes but most editors amend
this to Polixenes.

148–149 You look As...distraction: your wrinkled forehead
suggests that you are deeply worried. 'Brow' is another
ironic reference to horns.

150 moved: angry
in good earnest: seriously

151–153 How sometimes...bosoms!: sometimes affection (fo
one's children) will show itself in silly or tender behaviour
which entertains the dispassionate observer

155 Twenty-three years: suggesting Leontes is aged about 30
unbreeched: too young to wear breeches

159–160 this kernel, This squash: this soft child, this unripe
pea-pod; both images suggest a lack of the hard exterior
which comes with maturity

161 Will you...money?: a proverb meaning 'Will you allow
yourself to be cheated?' Here, 'for' means 'instead of'.

163 happy man be's dole: may you live to be happy

165 seem: appear
If at home: when I am at home

166 He's all my exercise: I spend all my spare time with him

> • *In what ways is Leontes' reply to Hermione ironic?*
> *What is significant in the imagery he uses?*

> dost,
> (And that beyond commission) and I find it,
> (And that to the infection of my brains   145
> And hard'ning of my brows).

POLIXENES
                                          What means Sicilia?

HERMIONE   He something seems unsettled.

POLIXENES
                                          How, my lord?
What cheer? How is't with you, best brother?

HERMIONE
                                          You look
As if you held a brow of much distraction:
Are you moved, my lord?

LEONTES
                                          No, in good earnest.   150
How sometimes nature will betray its folly,
Its tenderness, and make itself a pastime
To harder bosoms! Looking on the lines
Of my boy's face, methoughts I did recoil
Twenty-three years, and saw myself unbreeched, 155
In my green velvet coat; my dagger muzzled
Lest it should bite its master, and so prove,
As ornaments oft do, too dangerous:
How like, methought, I then was to this kernel,
This squash, this gentleman. Mine honest
      friend,   160
Will you take eggs for money?

MAMILLIUS   No, my lord, I'll fight.

LEONTES   You will? Why, happy man be's dole! My brother,
Are you so fond of your young prince, as we
Do seem to be of ours?

POLIXENES
                                          If at home, sir,   165
He's all my exercise, my mirth, my matter:
Now my sworn friend, and then mine enemy;
My parasite, my soldier, statesman, all.
He makes a July's day short as December;
And with his varying childness cures in me   170

Having emphasized their affection for their sons, the kings separate. Leontes remains with Mamillius and instructs Hermione to entertain Polixenes as generously as is possible. As she and the rest of the court leave, Leontes reveals that he is attempting to trap Hermione and Polixenes.

171 **thick my blood**: sadden me; make me melancholy

171–172 **So stands...with me**: this is the duty I require of my son (who attends me like a squire)

174 **How thou lov'st...welcome**: demonstrate your love for me through your hospitality towards Polixenes

177 **Apparent to my heart**: the heir to my love

178 **shall 's attend you there?**: shall we wait for you there?

179 **To your own bents dispose you**: do whatever you have an inclination to

180–181 **angling, line**: Leontes perceives himself as a fisherman attempting to catch his wife and Polixenes

183 **neb, bill**: beak, mouth

186 **Inch-thick**: solid, like a plank of wood, and thus undoubted
a forked one: Leontes alludes to his cuckold's horns, to Hermione's deceit and the forks of the legs. This is the first of a series of savage sexual images.

187–188 **play**: the word describes, in turn, child's play, sexual games, and acting.

188 **issue**: exit, here of a failed actor, but also perhaps meaning 'child' and thus the first suggestion that Leontes suspects that Hermione is pregnant by Polixenes

190 **knell**: death bell

191 **ere**: before

194 **sluiced**: the action of drawing water from a lake, usually through a gate and channel. The image suggests pond in the next line, and gate in line197.

> • *What is your reaction to Leontes' attempt to entrap Hermione and Polixenes?*

Thoughts that would thick my blood.

LEONTES   So stands this squire
Officed with me. We two will walk, my lord,
And leave you to your graver steps. Hermione,
How thou lov'st us, show in our brother's
   welcome;
Let what is dear in Sicily be cheap: 175
Next to thyself, and my young rover, he's
Apparent to my heart.

HERMIONE   If you would seek us,
We are yours i' th' garden: shall 's attend you there?

LEONTES To your own bents dispose you: you'll be found,
Be you beneath the sky. [*Aside*] I am angling
   now,   180
Though you perceive me not how I give line.
Go to, go to!
How she holds up the neb, the bill to him!
And arms her with the boldness of a wife
To her allowing husband!
                [*Exeunt* POLIXENES *and* HERMIONE
                    Gone already!   185
Inch-thick, knee-deep; o'er head and ears a forked
   one.
Go, play, boy, play: thy mother plays, and I
Play too; but so disgraced a part, whose issue
Will hiss me to my grave: contempt and clamour
Will be my knell. Go, play, boy, play. There have
   been,   190
(Or I am much deceived) cuckolds ere now,
And many a man there is (even at this present,
Now, while I speak this) holds his wife by th' arm,
That little thinks she has been sluiced in 's absence
And his pond fished by his next neighbour, by 195
Sir Smile, his neighbour: nay, there's comfort in't,
Whiles other men have gates, and those gates
   opened,

Leontes becomes obsessed by his wife's supposed sexual
infidelity, imagining it to be the common experience of
husbands. When Camillo enters, Leontes dismisses his son
and begins to question the courtier on the reasons for
Polixenes' decision to extend his visit. Camillo does not
suspect that he is being manipulated.

200 Physic: medicine
201–202 It is a bawdy...predominant: an unfaithful wife is like
   the planet of love and lust, Venus, influencing the lives of
   men where and how she pleases. 'Strike' and 'predominant'
   are astrological terms.
202 think it: be assured of it
204 No barricado for a belly: there's no way of preventing
   entry to a womb. Barricado – barrier – is a military term and
   thus suggests the following two lines.
208 some comfort: because it suggests that Mamillius is
   legitimate
211 an honest man: perhaps this refers both to Mamillius'
   legitimacy and Camillo's character
212 Sir: used ironically, as also in line 196
213–214 You had much...home: whenever you tried to anchor
   him here the anchor dragged and he was in danger of going
   away
218 so-forth: euphemism for cuckold
218–219 'Tis far...last: it (the rumour) must have been current
   for a long time since the cuckold always hears it last. Gust,
   meaning taste, is used metaphorically.
221–222 At the queen's...not: just say the queen; 'good'
   should be appropriate but, as things are, it isn't
222 taken: noticed
223 pate: head
224–225 For thy conceit...blocks: your understanding soaks
   up, like a sponge, more than common blockheads

- *Comment on Leontes' imagery. What does it indicate
  about his state of mind?*
- *How does Camillo unintentionally add to Leontes'
  misery?*

As mine, against their will. Should all despair
That have revolted wives, the tenth of mankind
Would hang themselves. Physic for't there's
   none;   200
It is a bawdy planet, that will strike
Where 'tis predominant; and 'tis powerful, think it,
From east, west, north, and south; be it concluded,
No barricado for a belly. Know 't,
It will let in and out the enemy,   205
With bag and baggage: many thousand on 's
Have the disease, and feel 't not. How now, boy?

MAMILLIUS   I am like you, they say.

LEONTES   Why, that's some comfort.
What, Camillo there?

CAMILLO   Ay, my good lord.   210

LEONTES   Go play, Mamillius; thou'rt an honest man.
                               [*Exit* MAMILLIUS
Camillo, this great Sir will yet stay longer.

CAMILLO   You had much ado to make his anchor hold:
When you cast out, it still came home.

LEONTES   Didst note it?

CAMILLO   He would not stay at your petitions; made   215
His business more material.

LEONTES   Didst perceive it?
[*Aside*] They're here with me already; whisp'ring,
   rounding
'Sicilia is a so-forth'. 'Tis far gone,
When I shall gust it last. – How came 't, Camillo,
That he did stay?

CAMILLO   At the good queen's entreaty. 220

LEONTES   At the queen's be 't: 'good' should be pertinent,
But so it is, it is not. Was this taken
By any understanding pate but thine?
For thy conceit is soaking, will draw in

Leontes begins to reveal his feelings and suspicions to
Camillo. When Camillo shows himself unaware of
Hermione's infidelity, Leontes accuses him of either deceit or
stupidity.

225-226 Not noted...natures?: is it only observed by the more
    sensitive upper classes?

226 severals: individuals

227-228 Lower messes...purblind?: the people of lower social
    rank who eat at my table are perhaps blind to the queen's
    behaviour?

237-239 My chamber-counsels...reformed: Camillo is
    portrayed as Leontes' closest personal adviser, almost like a
    priest who would hear a confession and absolve the guilty
    person of their sins

242 To bide upon 't: to insist on my point

244-245 hoxes honesty...required: hamstrings honesty,
    cutting it down from behind, as one might force a horse
    from its true course

245 or else: either

246 grafted in my serious trust: intimately concerned with my
    confidential affairs (like a branch grafted to a tree)

247-249 or else a fool...jest: or you are a fool who watches a
    skilful player win other people's money and just laughs at
    the consequences

252 But that: except that

> • *What details here contrast with the mood established in
> the first scene of the play?*

	More than the common blocks. Not noted, is't, 225
	But of the finer natures? By some severals
	Of head-piece extraordinary? Lower messes
	Perchance are to this business purblind? Say!
CAMILLO	Business, my lord? I think most understand
	Bohemia stays here longer.
LEONTES	Ha?
CAMILLO	Stays here longer. 230
LEONTES	Ay, but why?
CAMILLO	To satisfy your highness, and the entreaties
	Of our most gracious mistress.
LEONTES	Satisfy?
	Th' entreaties of your mistress? Satisfy?
	Let that suffice. I have trusted thee, Camillo, 235
	With all the nearest things to my heart, as well
	My chamber-counsels, wherein, priest-like, thou
	Hast cleansed my bosom: I from thee departed
	Thy penitent reformed. But we have been
	Deceived in thy integrity, deceived 240
	In that which seems so.
CAMILLO	Be it forbid, my lord!
LEONTES	To bide upon 't: thou art not honest: or,
	If thou inclin'st that way, thou art a coward,
	Which hoxes honesty behind, restraining
	From course required: or else thou must be counted 245
	A servant grafted in my serious trust,
	And therein negligent; or else a fool,
	That seest a game played home, the rich stake drawn,
	And tak'st it all for jest.
CAMILLO	My gracious lord,
	I may be negligent, foolish, and fearful; 250
	In every one of these no man is free,
	But that his negligence, his folly, fear,

Camillo eloquently defends himself, claiming that he cannot comprehend Leontes. The king declares Hermione's unfaithfulness but Camillo refuses to believe it.

254 puts forth: is evident

255 wilful-negligent: intentionally neglectful

256 industriously: deliberately

258 Not weighing well the end: not adequately considering the outcome

258–262 if ever fearful...wisest: if I were ever afraid to act because I could not be sure of the result, even though there was an obvious need to do something, such fear is common enough amongst the wisest men

265–267 let me know...mine: tell me my error clearly, so that can recognize it; if I then deny knowing it, it is not a child of mine

268 eye-glass: lens of the eye

269 thicker: more impenetrable

270–271 (For to a...mute): because people are sure to talk about something so visible

271 cogitation: ability to think

273 slippery: unfaithful

273–275 If thou wilt...thought: admit you know; to claim to have seen, heard or thought nothing is impudent

276 a hobby-horse: an immoral woman – an unpleasant slang term which Leontes tries to justify in his next phrase

277 rank: morally corrupt
flax-wench: literally a girl who works with linen cloth and thus another disparaging social comparison

277–278 puts to...plight: has sexual intercourse before she is legally contracted to marry

280 clouded: blackened

281 present: immediate
'shrew: beshrew; the devil take

283–284 which to reiterate...true: to repeat what you have said would be as great a sin as that which you charge Hermione with, even if it were true

Among the infinite doings of the world,
Sometime puts forth. In your affairs, my lord,
If ever I were wilful-negligent,   255
It was my folly: if industriously
I played the fool, it was my negligence,
Not weighing well the end: if ever fearful
To do a thing, where I the issue doubted,
Whereof the execution did cry out   260
Against the non-performance, 'twas a fear
Which oft infects the wisest. These, my lord,
Are such allowed infirmities that honesty
Is never free of. But, beseech your Grace,
Be plainer with me; let me know my trespass   265
By its own visage: if I then deny it,
'Tis none of mine.

LEONTES   Ha' not you seen, Camillo
(But that's past doubt: you have, or your eye-glass
Is thicker than a cuckold's horn) or heard
(For to a vision so apparent rumour   270
Cannot be mute) or thought (for cogitation
Resides not in that man that does not think)
My wife is slippery? If thou wilt confess,
Or else be impudently negative,
To have nor eyes, nor ears, nor thought, then say   275
My wife's a hobby-horse, deserves a name
As rank as any flax-wench that puts to
Before her troth-plight: say't and justify 't!

CAMILLO I would not be a stander-by, to hear
My sovereign mistress clouded so, without   280
My present vengeance taken: 'shrew my heart,
You never spoke what did become you less
Than this; which to reiterate were sin
As deep as that, though true.

LEONTES   Is whispering nothing?

The king repeats his accusations, calls Camillo a liar and tel|
him that Polixenes is Hermione's lover.

287 **note**: sign
288 **Horsing**: to set; with an allusion to the further meaning o|
     stallion covering a mare
291 **the pin and web**: cataract, a disease of the eye which clou|
     sight
     but: except
292 **That would...wicked**: who wish to sin unnoticed
297 **betimes**: straight away
298 **Say it be, 'tis true**: it may be (dangerous) but it is true
302 **hovering temporizer**: waverer who can't make up his mi|
304 **liver**: considered to be the source of the passions
306 **The running...glass**: an hour; the time taken for the sand
     to run through an hour-glass
307 **medal**: medallion; miniature portrait
310–311 **To see alike...thrifts**: who could see the requireme|
     of my honour as clearly as they can see their own advantag
     and interests
312 **undo more doing**: make any further action impossible –
     that is, kill Polixenes
313–314 **from meaner...worship**: from a lower position have
     raised you to a high seat at court and to honour (compare
     'Lower messes' in line 227 above)

• *Comment on the imagery used by Camillo. Compare*
  what he says here with his speech on page 5. What
  conclusion do you draw?

Is leaning cheek and cheek? Is meeting noses?   285
Kissing with inside lip? Stopping the career
Of laughter with a sigh (a note infallible
Of breaking honesty)? Horsing foot on foot?
Skulking in corners? Wishing clocks more swift?
Hours, minutes? Noon, midnight? And all eyes   290
Blind with the pin and web, but theirs; theirs only.
That would unseen be wicked? Is this nothing?
Why then the world, and all that's in't, is nothing,
The covering sky is nothing, Bohemia nothing,
My wife is nothing, nor nothing have these
   nothings,   295
If this be nothing.

CAMILLO   Good my lord, be cured
Of this diseased opinion, and betimes,
For 'tis most dangerous.

LEONTES   Say it be, 'tis true.

CAMILLO   No, no, my lord.

LEONTES   It is: you lie, you lie:
I say thou liest, Camillo, and I hate thee,   300
Pronounce thee a gross lout, a mindless slave,
Or else a hovering temporizer that
Canst with thine eyes at once see good and evil,
Inclining to them both. Were my wife's liver
Infected, as her life, she would not live   305
The running of one glass.

CAMILLO   Who does infect her?

LEONTES   Why, he that wears her like her medal, hanging
About his neck, Bohemia; who, if I
Had servants true about me, that bare eyes
To see alike mine honour as their profits,   310
Their own particular thrifts, they would do that
Which should undo more doing: ay, and thou
His cupbearer, – whom I from meaner form
Have benched and reared to worship, who may'st
   see

Leontes challenges Camillo to murder Polixenes. When Camillo admits that he could do the deed but doesn't believe Hermione's guilt, Leontes angrily repeats his accusations. Camillo says that he 'must' believe the king and will kill Polixenes provided that Leontes will be reconciled to Hermione.

316 **galled**: made bitter and exasperated
   bespice a cup: flavour wine with spices – here a euphemism for poison
317 **a lasting wink**: eyes which are forever closed
318 **draught**: drink
   cordial: medicine
319 **rash**: quick-acting
320 **dram**: drink – used to describe a draught of medicine or poison
321 **Maliciously**: violently (and thus could not be detected)
322 **crack**: flaw
   dread mistress: my queen whom I hold in awe and reverence
323 **So sovereignly being honourable**: being so supremely honourable
324 **Make that...rot!**: if you question what I have said about Hermione, go to hell!
325 **so muddy, so unsettled**: so cloudy in judgement, mentally disturbed
326 **To appoint...vexation**: to clothe myself in this trouble
332 **ripe moving to 't**: immediate evidence available to prove it
333 **blench**: swerve (presumably from reason or good sense)
334 **fetch off**: kill – but in using this euphemism, and 'removed' in the next line, Camillo is implying a contrary course of action
336 **at first**: when you were first married
337–338 **for sealing...tongues**: stopping harmful rumours
343 **countenance as clear**: face as open

• *Do you think that Camillo is capable of murder? What reasons would he have for obeying Leontes and what would be his reasons for disobedience?*

Plainly as heaven sees earth and earth sees
    heaven,   315
How I am galled, – might'st bespice a cup,
To give mine enemy a lasting wink;
Which draught to me were cordial.

CAMILLO   Sir, my lord,
I could do this, and that with no rash potion,
But with a ling'ring dram, that should not work 320
Maliciously, like poison: but I cannot
Believe this crack to be in my dread mistress
(So sovereignly being honourable).
I have loved thee, –

LEONTES   Make that thy question, and go rot!
Dost think I am so muddy, so unsettled,   325
To appoint myself in this vexation; sully
The purity and whiteness of my sheets,
(Which to preserve is sleep, which being spotted
Is goads, thorns, nettles, tails of wasps)
Give scandal to the blood o' th' prince, my son, 330
(Who I do think is mine and love as mine)
Without ripe moving to 't? Would I do this?
Could man so blench?

CAMILLO   I must believe you, sir:
I do; and will fetch off Bohemia for't;
Provided, that when he's removed, your
    highness   335
Will take again your queen, as yours at first,
Even for your son's sake, and thereby for sealing
The injury of tongues in courts and kingdoms
Known and allied to yours.

LEONTES   Thou dost advise me
Even so as I mine own course have set down: 340
I'll give no blemish to her honour, none.

CAMILLO My lord,
Go then; and with a countenance as clear
As friendship wears at feasts, keep with Bohemia,

Leontes agrees to Camillo's terms, and exits. Camillo, in a soliloquy, recognizes Leontes' mental disorder and vows not to do the deed even though he must leave the court and risk his life. Polixenes enters and is disturbed at having been ignored by the departing Leontes.

345 cupbearer: the officer of a king's court who served his master with wine

353 ground: reason

355–356 will have All...too: wishes all his servants to share his mental turmoil

360 Nor...nor: neither...nor. The apparent double negative of the succeeding 'not' was a common means of giving emphasis.

362–363 to do 't...break-neck: whether I murder Polixenes or not I shall die for it (if I stay here)

363 Happy star reign now: compare lines 201–202. Camillo prays for an astrological conjunction which will ensure his good fortune.

364 This is strange: Polixenes has been ignored by the departing Leontes

365 warp: shrink

367 None rare: nothing unusual

> • *In what ways does the style used by Camillo in his soliloquy differ from that of his speech to Leontes on page 25?*

	And with your queen. I am his cupbearer: 345
	If from me he have wholesome beverage,
	Account me not your servant.
LEONTES	This is all:
	Do't, and thou hast the one half of my heart;
	Do't not, thou splitt'st thine own.
CAMILLO	I'll do't, my lord.
LEONTES	I will seem friendly, as thou hast advised me. 350

[*Exit*

CAMILLO O miserable lady! But, for me,
What case stand I in? I must be the poisoner
Of good Polixenes, and my ground to do 't
Is the obedience to a master; one
Who, in rebellion with himself, will have 355
All that are his so too. To do this deed,
Promotion follows. If I could find example
Of thousands that had struck anointed kings
And flourished after, I'd not do 't: but since
Nor brass, nor stone, nor parchment bears not
one, 360
Let villainy itself forswear't. I must
Forsake the court: to do 't, or no, is certain
To me a break-neck. Happy star reign now!
Here comes Bohemia.

Enter POLIXENES

POLIXENES [*Aside*] This is strange: methinks
My favour here begins to warp. Not speak? 365
Good day, Camillo.

CAMILLO Hail, most royal sir!

POLIXENES What is the news i' th' court?

CAMILLO None rare, my lord.

POLIXENES The king hath on him such a countenance
As he had lost some province, and a region
Loved as he loves himself: even now I met him 370

Polixenes begins to sound Camillo out. Camillo is circumspect in not revealing the cause of Leontes' strange behaviour but his answers invite Polixenes to ask further questions and the king realizes that he himself is at the root of the problem.

372–373 Wafting his...contempt: looking away and curling his lips contemptuously

374 what is breeding: what is developing

378 intelligent: intelligible

378–380 'tis thereabouts...dare not: that's what it is, since it is impossible not to know what you do know; you cannot say that you dare not know something

381 complexions: looks

382–84 for I must...with 't: Leontes' changed feelings toward me must be my fault since I feel myself affected by the change

385 in distemper: out of temper; unbalanced both physically and emotionally

388 basilisk: mythical beast which killed its victims by looking at them

392 Clerk-like: learned, perhaps with a suggestion of priestly qualities (see earlier, line 237)

392–394 which no less...gentle: learning is as important an attribute of nobility as are our family names which make us noble through inheritance

395–396 aught which...informed: anything which I should know

396–397 imprison 't not In ignorant concealment: don't keep it to yourself by pretending you don't know anything about it

400–402 I conjure...mine: I solemnly implore, by all the qualities of an honourable man, not the least of which is my demand that you answer me

- *What qualities does Polixenes demonstrate during this conversation?*
- *Comment on the irony of Polixenes' words.*
- *What imagery with which we are already familiar does Camillo use?*

	With customary compliment, when he,	
	Wafting his eyes to th' contrary, and falling	
	A lip of much contempt, speeds from me, and	
	So leaves me, to consider what is breeding	
	That changes thus his manners.	375
CAMILLO	I dare not know, my lord.	
POLIXENES	How, dare not? Do not? Do you know, and dare not?	
	Be intelligent to me: 'tis thereabouts:	
	For, to yourself, what you do know, you must,	
	And cannot say you dare not. Good Camillo,	380
	Your changed complexions are to me a mirror	
	Which shows me mine changed too; for I must be	
	A party in this alteration, finding	
	Myself thus altered with 't.	
CAMILLO	There is a sickness	
	Which puts some of us in distemper, but	385
	I cannot name the disease, and it is caught	
	Of you, that yet are well.	
POLIXENES	How caught of me?	
	Make me not sighted like the basilisk.	
	I have looked on thousands, who have sped the better	
	By my regard, but killed none so. Camillo, –	390
	As you are certainly a gentleman, thereto	
	Clerk-like experienced, which no less adorns	
	Our gentry than our parents' noble names,	
	In whose success we are gentle, – I beseech you,	
	If you know aught which does behove my knowledge	395
	Thereof to be informed, imprison 't not	
	In ignorant concealment.	
CAMILLO	I may not answer.	
POLIXENES	A sickness caught of me, and yet I well?	
	I must be answered. Dost thou hear, Camillo?	
	I conjure thee, by all the parts of man	400

Camillo is persuaded by Polixenes that it is honourable for him to reveal what he knows. He tells Polixenes that he has been appointed his murderer. Polixenes vehemently denies adultery with Hermione. Camillo tells Polixenes that Leontes is unshakable in his belief that Hermione has betrayed him and that it is pointless to consider how this has come about.

403 incidency: future event

405 if to be: if that is possible

412 him: the person

415 As he had: as if he had

415–416 an instrument...to 't: an instrument of torture to force you (either to commit adultery or to confess that you had done)

419 his that...Best!: Judas that betrayed Jesus

421 A savour...nostril: a bad odour that even someone with little sense of smell could detect. It was believed that smells were a sign of disease.

424–426 Swear his thought...influences: deny what he is thinking and swear by all the stars in heaven and their effects on humanity

428–431 As or by...body: as either by an oath or good advice shake the building he has created from his foolishness, since its foundations are a matter of belief and will last as long as his human body

- *Look at the rhythm of this exchange between Polixenes and Camillo – the way in which the conversation flows between the two men. How does Shakespeare ensure a gathering pace and urgency?*

Which honour does acknowledge, whereof the least
Is not this suit of mine, that thou declare
What incidency thou dost guess of harm
Is creeping toward me; how far off, how near,
Which way to be prevented, if to be: 405
If not, how best to bear it.

CAMILLO   Sir, I will tell you;
Since I am charged in honour, and by him
That I think honourable. Therefore mark my
        counsel,
Which must be ev'n as swiftly followed as
I mean to utter it, or both yourself and me   410
Cry lost, and so good night!

POLIXENES   On, good Camillo.

CAMILLO   I am appointed him to murder you.

POLIXENES   By whom, Camillo?

CAMILLO   By the king.

POLIXENES   For what?

CAMILLO   He thinks, nay, with all confidence he swears,
As he had seen 't, or been an instrument   415
To vice you to't, that you have touched his queen
Forbiddenly.

POLIXENES   O then, my best blood turn
To an infected jelly, and my name
Be yoked with his that did betray the Best!
Turn then my freshest reputation to   420
A savour that may strike the dullest nostril
Where I arrive, and my approach be shunned,
Nay, hated too, worse than the great'st infection
That e'er was heard or read!

CAMILLO   Swear his thought over
By each particular star in heaven, and   425
By all their influences; you may as well
Forbid the sea for to obey the moon,
As or by oath remove or counsel shake

Camillo advises Polixenes to escape from the city, promises to assist his departure and to serve him in the future. Polixenes, accepting Camillo's help, seeks to explain Leontes' jealousy. He expresses his fear, his hopes for Hermione, and his respect of Camillo.

431 grow: have developed

435–436 this trunk...impawned: my body which you must take with you as a pledge of my honesty. Camillo puns on trunk. Both syllables of 'enclosed' should be stressed.

438 posterns: small city gates

443–446 which if you...sworn: if you try to prove the truth of what I have said (by speaking directly to Leontes), I shall deny my words and you will be no more secure than someone whom the king has condemned and sentenced to death. All syllables of condemned should be stressed.

448–449 thy places...neighbour mine: your position at court shall always be close to me

456 Professed: declared love

458–460 Good expedition...suspicion: may a speedy departure save me and help the queen, the subject of his anger but who has done nothing to justify his suspicions

> • *Camillo and Polixenes summarize Leontes' state of mind and the reasons for it. What do they conclude?*

The fabric of his folly, whose foundation
Is piled upon his faith, and will continue   430
The standing of his body.

POLIXENES   How should this grow?

CAMILLO   I know not: but I am sure 'tis safer to
Avoid what's grown than question how 'tis born.
If therefore you dare trust my honesty,
That lies enclosed in this trunk which you   435
Shall bear along impawned, away to-night!
Your followers I will whisper to the business,
And will by twos and threes, at several posterns,
Clear them o' th' city. For myself, I'll put
My fortunes to your service, which are here   440
By this discovery lost. Be not uncertain,
For by the honour of my parents, I
Have uttered truth: which if you seek to prove,
I dare not stand by; nor shall you be safer
Than one condemned by the king's own
      mouth,   445
Thereon his execution sworn.

POLIXENES   I do believe thee:
I saw his heart in 's face. Give me thy hand,
Be pilot to me, and thy places shall
Still neighbour mine. My ships are ready, and
My people did expect my hence departure   450
Two days ago. This jealousy
Is for a precious creature: as she's rare,
Must it be great; and, as his person's mighty,
Must it be violent; and, as he does conceive
He is dishonoured by a man which ever   455
Professed to him, why, his revenges must
In that be made more bitter. Fear o'ershades me:
Good expedition be my friend, and comfort
The gracious queen, part of his theme, but nothing
Of his ill-ta'en suspicion! Come, Camillo,   460
I will respect thee as a father if

Camillo urges Polixenes to depart immediately.

462 Hence! Let us avoid: Away! let us go
465 take the urgent hour: seize the moment; act now

Thou bear'st my life off. Hence! Let us avoid.

CAMILLO It is in mine authority to command
The keys of all the posterns: please your highness
To take the urgent hour. Come sir, away. [*Exeunt*
465

ACTIVITIES

Keeping track

Scene 1

1 In the opening lines, what differences does Archidamus remark on between the court of Bohemia and that of Sicilia?
2 What will the Bohemians do in order that the Sicilian visitors will not notice their lack of hospitality?
3 Why, according to Camillo, is the friendship between Leontes and Polixenes so strong?
4 What hopes do Archidamus and Camillo have for Mamillius?

Scene 2

1 What reasons does Polixenes give for having to leave Leontes' court?
2 In what ways does Hermione try to persuade Polixenes to stay (lines 34–56)?
3 Hermione is told that she has never spoken to better purpose.
   • What does Leontes mean?
   • On what other occasion did she use her power of speech well?
4 What is the first sign that Leontes is suspicious of Hermione?
5 What, according to Polixenes, are the joys of fatherhood?
6 • What does Leontes suspect about Polixenes' relationship with Hermione (lines 185–200)?
   • How is this then made more clear in his conversation with Camillo?
7 • What are the conditions on which Camillo will agree to poison Polixenes?
   • What are his private thoughts?
8 What are the reasons Polixenes gives to explain Leontes' rage?

Characters

As you study a play your perspectives on the characters will change. Keep notes of your reactions and the evidence on which they are based. These questions will help you to do this.

Leontes

1 What have we learned of the nature of the friendship between Leontes and Polixenes?
2 It is hard to account for his jealousy. Are there any indications of the reasons for its growth?
3 Is Leontes jealous before the play begins or is there one moment in Act 1 scene 2 when he begins to be suspicious for the first time?
4 If you were directing the actor playing Leontes in this act, what elements of his personality and internal thoughts would you try to emphasize? Are there any key words or phrases which you would work on with the actor?

Hermione

Hermione is quick-witted and articulate: Leontes says '*Well said, Hermione*' (scene 2 line 33). She is apparently in love with her husband: he says '*How thou lov'st us, show in our brother's welcome*' (scene 2 line 174). What other qualities does she possess? Find a quotation or other evidence for each one that you list.

Camillo

Camillo is engaged in three important conversations in this act – with Archidamus, with Leontes and with Polixenes.
1 Briefly summarize the main points of each.
2 What do we learn about his role at court?
3 What do we discover about his personal qualities?
4 He has been described as a loyal, honest servant. How far do you think this is accurate?

Polixenes

The king is not very fully drawn as a character. However, what he says about his friendship with Leontes is important.
1 What is the basis of their friendship?
2 What flaws are evident in it?

Themes

There are a number of ideas which seem to dominate Shakespeare's
thinking as he constructed this play.

1   Childhood. Polixenes and Leontes '*were trained together in their
    childhoods*' (scene 1 line 22). In what other ways have we been
    reminded of the importance of childhood and family life?
2   Friendship. '*To mingle friendship far, is mingling bloods*' (scene 2 line
    109). How has the fragile nature of friendship been explored?
3   Sexual jealousy. '*O, that is entertainment My bosom likes not, nor my
    brows*' (scene 2 lines 118–119). What is the impact of Leontes'
    jealousy on each of the principal characters so far?

Drama

1   As a group of six or more, look at scene 2 lines 60–86.
    Use FORUM THEATRE techniques (see page 263) to explore the
    physical positioning, moves and gestures possible during these lines:
    • two people read the words
    • three people act out the moves
    • the rest of the group become the directors suggesting different
      possibilities.
    Think about these points:
    • What is Leontes doing? (Signing papers? Talking to someone else?
      Is he sitting or standing or walking about? Is he watching
      Hermione and Polixenes surreptitiously or openly?)
    • Are Hermione and Polixenes touching? Are they flirting or are they
      completely innocent ? Is their conversation light or serious?
    • Consider the acting space. What areas would these three occupy?

2   In pairs, look at one or more of these speeches: '*Too hot! Too hot!...*'
    (scene 2 lines 108–119), '*Inch-thick, knee-deep...feel 't rot*' (scene 2
    lines 186–207) and '*Is whispering nothing...*' (scene 2 lines 284–296).
    • By saying the words and listening to each other, choose the ten or
      so words you enjoy saying the most. Many of these words are
      onomatopoeic or alliterative or both. They all show Leontes'
      boiling anger and accumulated hatred.
    • Find different ways of saying your favourite words, alter the tone
      and volume, emphasize particular sounds, e.g. the 's' sound in
      '*Sir Smile*' and '*sluic'd in 's absence*'.

3   • In pairs, imagine Leontes goes to a marriage guidance counsellor
      with his suspicions. Improvise the conversation.
    • Alternatively, working in threes, improvise a scene between
      Leontes, Hermione and the counsellor.

Close study

1 Scene 2 lines 267–278
Leontes is forced into telling Camillo exactly what he means. Read the
first sentence omitting the words in brackets (parentheses). Read it again
and include the words in parentheses.

- Which reading makes Leontes sound in control of himself?
- How does the material in the brackets change the rhythm of the
  speech?
- What does this structure suggest about Leontes' emotional state and
  the way that his mind is working?
- Look at the whole speech and note all the words or phrases that
  describe Hermione's sexual behaviour. What do they tell us about
  Leontes' attitude towards her?

2 Scene 2 lines 284–296
The speech is built around the verb 'is' and the noun 'nothing'.
Sometimes these words are left unsaid: e.g. '*(Is) horsing foot on foot
(nothing)?*'

- Count the number of times Leontes either says the word 'nothing'
  or leaves it unsaid.
- What is the significance of the repetition of this word?
- Why is the dramatic impact of the speech greater because some of
  the words are left for us to imagine?
- What does Leontes' repetition and use of rhetorical questions tell us
  about his state of mind?

Key scene

Scene 2 lines 108–208

Keying it in

1 This outburst of jealousy and suspicion is most unexpected.
   - What have we learned of the friendship between Polixenes and
     Leontes before this moment?
   - What impression have we received of Hermione before Leontes'
     outburst?
2 • What is Leontes doing during the conversation between Hermione
     and Polixenes (lines 34–86)?
   - Explain what Hermione is asking Leontes to make clear to her (lines
     90–101).
   - Look at Leontes' speeches between lines 86 and 105. What effects
     do Hermione's words have on Leontes' thoughts and mood?

The scene itself

3 Lines 109–119

- What is making Leontes suspicious?
- What do you notice about the way Leontes expresses his suspicions? (Comment, for example on the grammatical structure, his choice of words and their sounds.)

4 Lines 120–146

- Why does Leontes twice ask whether Mamillius is '*my boy*'?
- Summarize the sequence of Leontes' thoughts in this section.
- What problems did you have in trying to summarize Leontes? What do these problems indicate?
- Comment on the imagery that Leontes uses.

5 Lines 147–180

- Hermione does not help matters very much when she looks at her distraught husband and speaks of what she sees. What is significant about her words, and what is interesting about his reply?
- What has looking at his son made Leontes think about (lines 153–160)?
- In lines 162–177, why is Leontes pleased by Mamillius' reply?
- What does Polixenes say about his relationship with his son? What, do you think, is the mood and tone of Leontes' reply?

6 Lines 180–208

- In lines 180–183, what picture does Leontes create to describe the relationship between himself, Hermione and Polixenes?
- How is this picture developed in the section to line 196?
- What other images do you notice?
- How do you react to this imagery?
- How does the form and structure of Leontes' soliloquy emphasize his state of mind?
- In lines 196–202 Leontes takes cold comfort in his opinion that many husbands are cuckolds. Why, according to him, is there no remedy for that 'disease'?

Overview

7 This scene reveals the jealousy of Leontes.

- Do we understand the reasons for the suddenness and fury of Leontes' jealousy?
- How do you view the characters of Polixenes and Hermione? Are they to blame for Leontes' suspicions?

- In what ways would you expect this scene to be the key to the drama that follows?
- If you were staging this scene, what would your key considerations be in positioning and moving the actors?

Writing

1 Imagine that, as Camillo arranges the departure of Polixenes and himself, he meets Archidamus. Suppose that he explains his feelings about the situation and comments on Leontes' behaviour. Write what he says.

2 You are a psychiatrist who has been asked to interview Leontes on the subject of his jealousy. Write the dialogue between yourself and Leontes in which you attempt to explore the relationship that Leontes has had with Hermione before the events of the play begin and the change in that relationship during the course of Act 1.

3 Describe the relationship between Polixenes and Leontes and the way in which it changes in the course of the play so far.

4 Both Polixenes and Leontes make judgements about Camillo's behaviour and character. What do they say, and what is your considered opinion of him?

Hermione, perhaps tired from her advancing pregnancy, asks her ladies to entertain Mamillius. He makes some sharp, amusing comments about adult behaviour. The ladies comment upon Hermione's pregnancy.

8–11 **Your brows...pen**: Mamillius describes, and Shakespeare mocks, an aspect of the convention of female beauty
9 **so**: provided
11 **taught '**: taught you
16 **rounds apace**: grows large quickly (with her pregnancy)
18 **wanton**: play

> • *What mood is established here? What dramatic irony (see GLOSSARY page 269) is apparent in the situation?*

Act two

Scene 1

Enter HERMIONE, MAMILLIUS *and* LADIES

HERMIONE	Take the boy to you: he so troubles me,
	'Tis past enduring.

1ST LADY   Come, my gracious lord,
Shall I be your play-fellow?

MAMILLIUS   No, I'll none of you.

1ST LADY   Why, my sweet lord?

MAMILLIUS   You'll kiss me hard, and speak to me as if   5
I were a baby still. I love you better.

2ND LADY   And why so, my lord?

MAMILLIUS   Not for because
Your brows are blacker; yet black brows, they say,
Become some women best, so that there be not
Too much hair there, but in a semicircle,   10
Or a half-moon, made with a pen.

2ND LADY   Who taught ' this!

MAMILLIUS   I learned it out of women's faces. Pray now,
What colour are your eyebrows?

1ST LADY   Blue, my lord.

MAMILLIUS   Nay, that's a mock: I have seen a lady's nose
That has been blue, but not her eyebrows.

1ST LADY   Hark ye,   15
The queen your mother rounds apace: we shall
Present our services to a find new prince
One of these days, and then you'd wanton with us,
If we would have you.

2ND LADY   She is spread of late

Hermione asks Mamillius to tell her a story. Since it is winter he offers a sad ghost story. As he begins to whisper it to his mother, Leontes arrives. He is hearing a report of the flight of Polixenes and Camillo which he believes justifies his suspicions. His life, he observes, has been poisoned.

20 good time encounter her: may she encounter good fortune (in the birth of her child)

21 What wisdom...you: what are you talking about?

22 I am for you: I am ready for you

31 Yond crickets: the ladies, who are chattering like chirping crickets

35 scour: hurry
eyed: watched, spied upon

36–37 How blest...censure: what a blessing that my judgement is so good

38–39 Alack, for...blest!: If only I knew less! I am cursed by my own good judgement.

40 A spider: spiders were believed to be poisonous, but only if a victim saw the creature in the cup
steeped: soaked

44 gorge: stomach
45 hefts: retching

> • *The ironic tone continues with the conversation between Mamillius and Hermione. How does it raise the tension of this scene?*

Into a goodly bulk: good time encounter her! 20

HERMIONE   What wisdom stirs amongst you? Come, sir, now
I am for you again: 'pray you, sit by us,
And tell 's a tale.

MAMILLIUS   Merry, or sad, shall't be?

HERMIONE   As merry as you will.

MAMILLIUS   A sad tale's best for winter: I have one 25
Of sprites and goblins.

HERMIONE   Let's have that, good sir.
Come on, sit down, come on, and do your best
To fright me with your sprites: you're powerful at it.

MAMILLIUS   There was a man –

HERMIONE   Nay, come sit down: then on.

MAMILLIUS   Dwelt by a churchyard: I will tell it softly, 30
Yond crickets shall not hear it.

HERMIONE   Come on then,
And giv't me in mine ear.

Enter LEONTES, *with* ANTIGONUS, LORDS *and others*

LEONTES   Was he met there? his train? Camillo with him?

A LORD   Behind the tuft of pines I met them, never
Saw I men scour so on their way: I eyed them 35
Even to their ships.

LEONTES   How blest am I
In my just censure, in my true opinion!
Alack, for lesser knowledge – how accursed
In being so blest! There may be in the cup
A spider steeped, and one may drink, depart, 40
And yet partake no venom (for his knowledge
Is not infected); but if one present
Th' abhorred ingredient to his eye, make known
How he hath drunk, he cracks his gorge, his sides,
With violent hefts. I have drunk, and seen the
spider. 45

Enraged, Leontes snatches Mamillius from Hermione and sends him away. The King publicly charges Hermione with adultery: it is Polixenes, he says, who has made her pregnant.

46 pander: go-between, especially between lovers

48 All's true that is mistrusted: all that I suspected is true

50 He has discovered my design: Camillo has revealed my plan

51 pinched: tortured. Leontes plays on another sense, a childish hurt, which suggests the playing of tricks in the next clause. Trick also means toy.

54 Which often...so: which has often commanded in a similar way

56 Give me the boy: said to Hermione
   I am glad you did not nurse him: the implication is that Mamillius was not suckled by Hermione but by a wet-nurse. Though this was not an unusual practice, Leontes turns it to his purpose by suggesting that the boy has had none of her milk though he has inherited her blood.

58 sport: a game

62 I'd: I would; Hermione continues to think that Leontes is playing a game and she offers an answer suitable for a hypothetical situation

64 th' nayward: the contrary

69 without-door form: her outward, public appearance

70–73 straight The shrug...does: immediately shrug, cough or laugh and so slander her – but no, such small gestures would be a mercy

73–74 calumny will sear Virtue: even the best can be branded by slander; a piece of proverbial wisdom

Camillo was his help in this, his pander:
There is a plot against my life, my crown;
All's true that is mistrusted: that false villain,
Whom I employed, was pre-employed by him:
He has discovered my design, and I   50
Remain a pinched thing; yea, a very trick
For them to play at will. How came the posterns
So easily open?

A LORD   By his great authority,
Which often hath no less prevailed than so
On your command.

LEONTES   I know't too well.   55
Give me the boy: I am glad you did not nurse him:
Though he does bear some signs of me, yet you
Have too much blood in him.

HERMIONE   What is this? sport?

LEONTES   Bear the boy hence, he shall not come about her,
Away with him, and let her sport herself   60
With that she's big with; for 'tis Polixenes
Has made thee swell thus. [*Exit* MAMILLIUS,
                                 accompanied by a LADY

HERMIONE   But I'd say he had not;
And I'll be sworn you would believe my saying,
How e'er you lean to th' nayward.

LEONTES   You, my lords,
Look on her, mark her well: be but about   65
To say 'she is a goodly lady,' and
The justice of your hearts will thereto add
' 'Tis pity she's not honest, honourable':
Praise her but for this her without-door form
(Which on my faith deserves high speech) and
          straight   70
The shrug, the hum or ha, these petty brands
That calumny doth use – O, I am out,
That mercy does; for calumny will sear
Virtue itself – these shrugs, these hum's and ha's,

Despite Hermione's denials, Leontes continues his invective against her.

79 **replenished**: complete
80 **He were as much more villain**: he would be twice as villainous
83 **Which I'll not...place**: I'll not call someone of your rank by a name appropriate to your behaviour
84 **barbarism**: the common people
85 **degrees**: social ranks
86 **mannerly distinguishment**: well-mannered distinctions
90 **federary**: confederate, accomplice
92 **But**: except
   principal: partner in crime – that is, Polixenes
93 **bed-swerver**: adulterer
94 **That vulgars...titles**: that the common people refer to with coarsest names
94–95 **privy To**: having secret knowledge of and being an accessory to
98 **published**: publicly slandered
99 **You scarce...throughly**: you will hardly be able thoroughly to restore my reputation
101 **foundations**: compare Act 1 scene 2 line 429
102 **The centre**: the earth, the centre of the universe according to the Ptolemaic description
104–105 **is afar off...speaks**: is indirectly guilty himself because he speaks

> • *Examine the language of this exchange. Why do we sympathize more with Hermione than with Leontes?*

When you have said 'she's goodly', come
    between,   75
Ere you can say 'she's honest': but be't known,
From him that has most cause to grieve it should
    be,
She's an adultress!

HERMIONE   Should a villain say so
(The most replenished villain in the world)
He were as much more villain: you, my lord,   80
Do but mistake.

LEONTES   You have mistook, my lady,
Polixenes for Leontes. O thou thing –
Which I'll not call a creature of thy place,
Lest barbarism, making me the precedent,
Should a like language use to all degrees,   85
And mannerly distinguishment leave out
Betwixt the prince and beggar. I have said
She's an adultress; I have said with whom:
More; she's a traitor, and Camillo is
A federary with her, and one that knows,   90
What she should shame to know herself
But with her most vile principal, that she's
A bed-swerver, even as bad as those
That vulgars give bold'st titles; ay, and privy
To this their late escape.

HERMIONE   No, by my life,   95
Privy to none of this. How will this grieve you,
When you shall come to clearer knowledge, that
You thus have published me? Gentle my lord,
You scarce can right me throughly, then, to say
You did mistake.

LEONTES   No: if I mistake   100
In those foundations which I build upon,
The centre is not big enough to bear
A school-boy's top. Away with her, to prison!
He who shall speak for her is afar off guilty

Leontes commands that Hermione be imprisoned. She accepts his decree with patience and dignity. Asking for her ladies to accompany her, she leaves. Antigonus and another lord intercede with Leontes on her behalf.

105 some ill planet reigns: compare Act 1 scene 2 lines 201–203. The planets were seen to wander in the night sky and their power to influence human fate varied according to their position in different constellations. Patience would thus see out the reign of an ill planet.

109–110 the want...pities: the lack of pointless tears will perhaps dry your sympathy for me

111 here: that is, in her heart

113–114 so qualified...measure me: so tempered as your love for me shall cause them to be, judge me

116 goes with me: accompanies me (to prison)

118 good fools: that is, her ladies

121 action: a play on the word which may imply a legal action, a military campaign and a theatrical role

122 better grace: see Act 1 scene 2 lines 99–105 and note. The sense here also suggests opposition to the 'disgrace' of prison.

131 Please you t': if it pleases you to

- *In what ways is Leontes seen to be losing credibility? How would stage business – gestures and physical actions – and the movements of the actors underline this?*

But that he speaks.

HERMIONE   There's some ill planet reigns: 105
I must be patient till the heavens look
With an aspect more favourable. Good my lords,
I am not prone to weeping, as our sex
Commonly are; the want of which vain dew
Perchance shall dry your pities: but I have   110
That honourable grief lodged here which burns
Worse than tears drown. Beseech you all, my lords,
With thoughts so qualified as your charities
Shall best instruct you, measure me; and so
The king's will be performed.

LEONTES   Shall I be heard?   115

HERMIONE   Who is't that goes with me? Beseech your
                highness,
My women may be with me, for you see
My plight requires it. Do not weep, good fools,
There is no cause: when you shall know your
                mistress
Has deserved prison, then abound in tears   120
As I come out: this action I now go on
Is for my better grace. Adieu, my lord:
I never wished to see you sorry; now
I trust I shall. My women, come; you have leave.

LEONTES   Go, do our bidding: hence!   125
                [*Exit* QUEEN, *guarded; with* LADIES

A LORD   Beseech your highness, call the queen again.

ANTIGONUS   Be certain what you do, sir, lest your justice
Prove violence, in the which three great ones suffer,
Yourself, your queen, your son.

A LORD   For her, my lord,
I dare my life lay down, and will do't, sir,   130
Please you t' accept it, that the queen is spotless
I' th' eyes of heaven, and to you – I mean
In this which you accuse her.

ANTIGONUS   If it prove

Antigonus pleads passionately on Hermione's behalf: she is, he says, the most virtuous of all women. Neither Antigonus nor the other Lord will believe Leontes' assertions.

134–136 I'll keep...trust her: I'll lock up my wife as I do my mares (away from the stallions): she and I will go leashed together like a pair of hounds; I'll not trust her further than I can touch and see her.

138 dram: morsel. A dram was a measure of weight equal to one-sixteenth of an ounce – less than two grammes.

141 You are abused...putter-on: you are deceived by some schemer. This, and the clause that follows, are ironic since Leontes is his own victim.

143 land-damn: this construction is unknown and now difficult to explain but the context and the metrical and onomatopoeic force are unmistakable: Antigonus would beat the life out of him
Be she honour-flawed: if her reputation should be damaged

145 The second...five: the second child is nine and the third is about five years old

147 I'll geld 'em all: I'll remove their ovaries, spay them. Antigonus refers again to horses: mares can be made infertile in this way.

148 false generations: both illegitimate children and children who themselves would be untrustworthy
co-heirs: equal beneficiaries of my estate

149 glib: castrate

150 fair issue: the opposite of 'false generations' (line 148)

153–154 As you feel...feel: there must be some appropriate stage business here: perhaps Leontes physically assaults Antigonus

157 dungy: unclean
lack I credit?: don't you believe me?

159 Upon this ground: on this issue

161 Be blamed...might: however you might be blamed for your error

- *How does the language used by Antigonus provide clues to his character?*

	She's otherwise, I'll keep my stables where
	I lodge my wife; I'll go in couples with her; 135
	Than when I feel and see her no farther trust her:
	For every inch of woman in the world,
	Ay, every dram of woman's flesh is false,
	If she be.
LEONTES	Hold your peaces.
A LORD	Good my lord, –
ANTIGONUS	It is for you we speak, not for ourselves: 140
	You are abused, and by some putter-on
	That will be damned for 't: would I knew the villain,
	I would land-damn him. Be she honour-flawed,
	I have three daughters: the eldest is eleven;
	The second and the third, nine and some five: 145
	If this prove true, they'll pay for 't. By mine honour
	I'll geld 'em all; fourteen they shall not see
	To bring false generations: they are co-heirs,
	And I had rather glib myself, than they
	Should not produce fair issue.
LEONTES	Cease; no more. 150
	You smell this business with a sense as cold
	As is a dead man's nose: but I do see 't and feel 't,
	As you feel doing thus; and see withal
	The instruments that feel.
ANTIGONUS	If it be so,
	We need no grave to bury honesty: 155
	There's not a grain of it the face to sweeten
	Of the whole dungy earth.
LEONTES	What! lack I credit?
A LORD	I had rather you did lack than I, my lord,
	Upon this ground: and more it would content me
	To have her honour true than your suspicion, 160
	Be blamed for 't how you might.
LEONTES	Why, what need we

Leontes dismisses the advice, repeats his grounds for suspicion but tells the courtiers that he has sent messengers, Cleomenes and Dion, to the temple of Apollo in order to obtain spiritual guidance. Leontes is convinced that he is right to have imprisoned Hermione and that the Oracle will vindicate him.

163 instigation: spur to action

163–64 Our prerogative...counsels: my power as sovereign does not require your advice

164 natural goodness: as an anointed king Leontes considers himself to be 'good' by virtue of his birth and position

165–167 which if you...like us: in respect of which, if you are either stupid or skilfully pretend to be so and thus cannot or will not appreciate a truth as I do

169 on 't: of it

172 more overture: making it public

175–179 their familiarity...th' deed: their intimacy, which was as obvious as any which ever served to prove a suspicion, that lacked only eye-witness evidence, that needed nothing to prove it except itself – circumstantial evidence proving that the deed had taken place

181–182 'twere Most piteous...wild: it would arouse great pity to act rashly

183 Delphos: Shakespeare follows Greene's *Pandosto* and other contemporary texts in confusing the island of Delos, where Apollo was born and worshipped, with the famous oracle at Delphi on the Greek mainland (see also Act 3 scene 1 line 2)

185 Of stuffed sufficiency: are very able

Oracle: a place where mortals were able to consult the gods of Ancient Greece

186 all: all that we need to know

191 he: presumably Antigonus

194 From our free person: away from my accessible body

Commune with you of this, but rather follow
Our forceful instigation? Our prerogative
Calls not your counsels, but our natural goodness
Imparts this; which if you, or stupefied,   165
Or seeming so, in skill, cannot or will not
Relish a truth, like us, inform yourselves
We need no more of your advice: the matter,
The loss, the gain, the ord'ring on 't, is all
Properly ours.

ANTIGONUS   And I wish, my liege,   170
You had only in your silent judgement tried it,
Without more overture.

LEONTES   How could that be?
Either thou art most ignorant by age,
Or thou wert born a fool. Camillo's flight,
Added to their familiarity,   175
(Which was as gross as ever touched conjecture,
That lacked sight only, nought for approbation
But only seeing, all other circumstances
Made up to th' deed) doth push on this
    proceeding.
Yet, for a greater confirmation   180
(For in an act of this importance, 'twere
Most piteous to be wild), I have dispatched in post
To sacred Delphos, to Apollo's temple,
Cleomenes and Dion, whom you know
Of stuffed sufficiency: now from the Oracle   185
They will bring all; whose spiritual counsel had,
Shall stop or spur me. Have I done well?

A LORD   Well done, my lord.

LEONTES   Though I am satisfied, and need no more
Than what I know, yet shall the Oracle   190
Give rest to th' minds of others; such as he
Whose ignorant credulity will not
Come up to th' truth. So have we thought it good
From our free person she should be confined,

Leontes intends to speak publicly of what has happened but Antigonus is sceptical.

198 raise: rouse

Some time later Paulina, wife of Antigonus, arrives at the prison to visit Hermione. The Gaoler will not let her in.

2 Let him have knowledge: inform him
8 To the contrary...commandment: I have a clear instruction that I may not (allow you to visit the queen)
9 ado: a to-do, a fuss
11 gentle: high-ranking
13–14 So please you...attendants: if you will, madam, send your attendants away

> • *What conflicting feelings about Leontes will the audience be experiencing by the end of Act 2 scene 1?*

Lest that the treachery of the two fled hence 195
Be left her to perform. Come, follow us;
We are to speak in public; for this business
Will raise us all.

ANTIGONUS   [*Aside*] To laughter, as I take it,
If the good truth were known.   [*Exeunt*

Scene 2

Enter PAULINA, *a* GENTLEMAN *and* ATTENDANTS

PAULINA   The keeper of the prison, call to him;
Let him have knowledge who I am. Good lady,
No court in Europe is too good for thee;
What dost thou then in prison?

Enter GAOLER

               Now good sir,
You know me, do you not?

GAOLER   For a worthy lady 5
And one who much I honour.

PAULINA   Pray you then,
Conduct me to the queen.

GAOLER   I may not, madam:
To the contrary I have express commandment.

PAULINA   Here's ado,
To lock up honesty and honour from 10
Th' access of gentle visitors! Is't lawful, pray you,
To see her women? any of them? Emilia?

GAOLER   So please you, madam,
To put apart these your attendants, I
Shall bring Emilia forth.

PAULINA   I pray now, call her. 15
Withdraw yourselves.

The Gaoler fetches Emilia, Hermione's lady-in-waiting, who reports that the queen has prematurely given birth to a daughter. Paulina announces that she will confront the king with the baby if Hermione will permit her. She hopes that the sight of his daughter will mitigate Leontes' anger.

19–20 Here's such ado...colouring: here is such an effort (to make innocence into guilt) as surpasses any craftsman's ability. Paulina puns on stain and also on colour which can mean 'to give credence' and 'to excuse'. See also Leontes: A 1 scene 2 line 132.

23 on: as a consequence of

24 greater: that is, the frights and griefs could not have been greater

27 like: likely

30 unsafe lunes i' th' king: treacherous madness of the king. Lunes, from the Latin *luna*, the moon, refers to intermittent insanity believed to have been brought about by the moon's changes.

33 honey-mouthed: sweet talking
let my tongue blister: it was proverbial that a liar's tongue blistered

35 trumpet: trumpeter. The image here suggests the trumpeter who announces the angry herald bringing a message of defiance on a battlefield.

38–39 to be Her advocate...loud'st: to speak on her behalf at the top of my voice

[*Exeunt* GENTLEMAN *and* ATTENDANTS

GAOLER   And, madam,
I must be present at your conference.

PAULINA   Well: be 't so: prithee.   [*Exit* GAOLER
Here's such ado to make no stain a stain
As passes colouring.

Enter GAOLER, *with* EMILIA

                              Dear gentlewoman,   20
How fares our gracious lady?

EMILIA   As well as one so great and so forlorn
May hold together: on her frights and griefs
(Which never tender lady hath borne greater)
She is, something before her time, delivered.   25

PAULINA   A boy?

EMILIA   A daughter; and a goodly babe,
Lusty, and like to live: the queen receives
Much comfort in 't; says, 'My poor prisoner,
I am innocent as you.'

PAULINA   I dare be sworn:
These dangerous, unsafe lunes i' th' king,
      beshrew them!   30
He must be told on 't, and he shall. The office
Becomes a woman best. I'll take 't upon me:
If I prove honey-mouthed, let my tongue blister,
And never to my red-looked anger be
The trumpet any more. Pray you, Emilia,   35
Commend my best obedience to the queen:
If she dares trust me with her little babe,
I'll show 't the King, and undertake to be
Her advocate to th' loud'st. We do not know
How he may soften at the sight o' th' child: 40
The silence often of pure innocence
Persuades, when speaking fails.

Emilia approves the idea but the Gaoler is worried that he has no permission to allow the baby out of prison. Paulina claims that natural justice is on her side and the Gaoler relents. She says that she will protect him.

44 free: generous

45 thriving issue: successful result

46 meet: suitable

47 presently: immediately (at this present time)

49 hammered of this design: deliberated urgently about such a plan

50 tempt a minister of honour: risk asking one of the king's close advisers

52 that tongue I have: all the rhetorical skill that I have

52–53 if wit flow...bosom: if the wisdom that flows from my mouth matches my heart's courage

55 come something nearer: to the queen; see line 47 above

63 If any be: if there is any guilt

trespass: sin

66 betwixt: between

> • *How are Paulina's firmness and clarity of purpose underlined by the way in which she speaks?*

EMILIA   Most worthy madam,
> Your honour and your goodness is so evident,
> That your free undertaking cannot miss
> A thriving issue: there is no lady living   45
> So meet for this great errand. Please your ladyship
> To visit the next room, I'll presently
> Acquaint the queen of your most noble offer,
> Who but to-day hammered of this design,
> But durst not tempt a minister of honour,   50
> Lest she should be denied.

PAULINA   Tell her, Emilia,
> I'll use that tongue I have: if wit flow from 't
> As boldness from my bosom, let 't not be doubted
> I shall do good.

EMILIA   Now be you blest for it!
> I'll to the queen: please you, come something
>   nearer.   55

GAOLER Madam, if 't please the queen to send the babe,
> I know not what I shall incur to pass it,
> Having no warrant.

PAULINA   You need not fear it, sir:
> This child was prisoner to the womb, and is
> By law and process of great nature, thence   60
> Freed and enfranchised; not a party to
> The anger of the king, nor guilty of
> (If any be) the trespass of the queen.

GAOLER I do believe it.

PAULINA Do not you fear: upon mine honour, I   65
> Will stand betwixt you and danger.   [*Exeunt*

Leontes is sleepless and distraught. Unable to punish
Polixenes he imagines that the death of Hermione would
restore his rest. A servant enters and we learn that Mamillius
is languishing as a result of Hermione's disgrace. Leontes
plans to revenge himself upon his queen.

4 **harlot**: immoral. The word was used of both sexes in
   Shakespeare's time.
5–6 **blank And level**: target and range (terms taken from
   gunnery)
6 **plot-proof**: safe from all my scheming
7 **hook to me**: deal with – the metaphor refers to the use of
   grappling irons by ships in battle and is suggested by 'blank
   and level' above. See also Leontes' angling images in Act 1
   scene 2 lines 180 and 195.
8 **the fire**: death by burning was a punishment for women
   guilty of treason
   a moiety: half
10 **the boy**: Mamillius
17 **solely**: alone
18 **him**: Polixenes
21 **parties**: allies
21–22 **let him be...serve**: leave him alone until an appropriate
   moment
24 **pastime**: entertainment

- *Leontes reveals his mental instability through the*
  language, structure and rhythm of his speeches. What
  words emphasize the violence of Leontes' thoughts?

cene 3

Enter LEONTES

LEONTES   Nor night, nor day, no rest: it is but weakness
To bear the matter thus: mere weakness. If
The cause were not in being, – part o' th' cause,
She th' adultress: for the harlot king
Is quite beyond mine arm, out of the blank   5
And level of my brain: plot-proof: but she
I can hook to me. Say that she were gone,
Given to the fire, a moiety of my rest
Might come to me again.

Enter SERVANT

                                        Who's there?

SERVANT   My Lord!

LEONTES   How does the boy?

SERVANT   He took good rest to-night; 10
'Tis hoped his sickness is discharged.

LEONTES   To see his nobleness!
Conceiving the dishonour of his mother
He straight declined, drooped, took it deeply,
Fastened and fixed the shame on 't in himself,   15
Threw off his spirit, his appetite, his sleep,
And downright languished. Leave me solely: go,
See how he fares.   [*Exit* SERVANT
                        Fie, fie! no thought of him:
The very thought of my revenges that way
Recoil upon me: in himself too mighty,   20
And in his parties, his alliance; let him be
Until a time may serve. For present vengeance,
Take it on her. Camillo and Polixenes
Laugh at me; make their pastime at my sorrow:
They should not laugh if I could reach them, nor 25

Paulina arrives with Hermione's baby. Neither Antigonus
nor anyone else can prevent her barging in on the king and
speaking about godparents for the baby. Leontes attacks
Antigonus for his weakness but Paulina asserts the honour of
her cause.

26 within: since she is within
27 second to: in support of
30 free: innocent
32 Not so hot: calm down
33–36 you, That creep...awaking: Paulina tells Leontes'
    servants that they merely echo his behaviour by creeping
    around like his shadows and thus increase – nourish – his
    suffering
35 heavings: sighs
38–39 to purge him...sleep: to rid him of the mental affliction
    which tortures him and stops him sleeping. The humours
    were the four chief fluids of the body – blood, phlegm, bile or
    choler, and black bile or melancholy – whose balance was
    thought to determine a person's physical and mental state.
    Illness, being 'out of humour', was often treated by changing
    this balance. Leeches could be used to reduce the amount of
    blood, and purgative drugs and emetics helped the body to
    lose the other fluids.
39 presses: pressing was a form of torture in which victims were
    pressed under heavy weights to extract confessions
41 gossips: godparents, for the baby's baptism
49 committing honour: committing sin is the normal usage but
    Paulina plays sarcastically upon the word

> • *What does Paulina say which makes her seem so*
> *forceful and in command of the situation?*

Shall she, within my power.

Enter PAULINA, *carrying a* BABY, *with* ANTIGONUS,
LORDS *and* SERVANTS, *who try to prevent her*

A LORD   You must not enter.

PAULINA   Nay rather, good my lords, be second to me:
Fear you his tyrannous passion more, alas
Than the queen's life? – a gracious innocent soul,
More free than he is jealous.

ANTIGONUS   That's enough.   30

SERVANT   Madam, he hath not slept to-night, commanded
None should come to him.

PAULINA   Not so hot, good sir;
I come to bring him sleep. 'Tis such as you,
That creep like shadows by him, and do sigh
At each his needless heavings; such as you   35
Nourish the cause of his awaking. I
Do come with words as medicinal as true,
Honest, as either, to purge him of that humour
That presses him from sleep.

LEONTES   What noise there, ho?

PAULINA   No noise, my lord, but needful conference   40
About some gossips for your highness.

LEONTES   How?
Away with that audacious lady! Antigonus,
I charged thee that she should not come about me.
I knew she would.

ANTIGONUS   I told her so, my lord,
On your displeasure's peril and on mine,   45
She should not visit you.

LEONTES   What! canst not rule her?

PAULINA   From all dishonesty he can: in this –
Unless he take the course that you have done,
Commit me for committing honour – trust it,
He shall not rule me.

Paulina proclaims Hermione's innocence. She threatens to scratch out the eyes of anyone who attempts to remove her from the Court and, laying the baby at Leontes' feet, asks for his blessing upon the child. Leontes is furious but cannot persuade any of his courtiers to remove Paulina.

50 La you now: there now

51 I let her run: Antigonus again compares his wife with his horses: see Act 2 scene 1 lines 134–135 and 147 for a similar comparison with his daughters

55–57 yet that dares...yours: yet I dare seem less than obedient in the way that I nurse you through your illness when compared with those who seem to be your most loyal servant

60 by combat...good: prove her virtue in a trial by combat, as a knight might fight for the honour of his lady. Compare her use of the word 'second' in line 27 above.

60–61 so were I...you: if I were a man, even though I were the worst at court

62–63 Let him that...I'll off: I'll scratch out the eyes of the first man that touches me; I'll go when I'm ready

67 mankind: masculine; virago

68 intelligencing bawd: pander – see Act 2 scene 1 line 46 and note

74 dotard: senile old man – directed at Antigonus

74–75 woman-tired, unroosted...here: henpecked, pushed off your perch by this foolish, noisy chicken. Partlet was the name of the hen in the fable of Reynard the Fox.

76 crone: old woman; broken-toothed old ewe

> • *Note the words used by Leontes to describe others. In what ways are they characteristic of the king?*

ANTIGONUS   La you now, you hear: 50
When she will take the rein I let her run;
But she'll not stumble.

PAULINA   Good my liege, I come, –
And, I beseech you hear me, who professes
Myself your loyal servant, your physician,
Your most obedient counsellor, yet that dares   55
Less appear so, in comforting your evils,
Than such as most seem yours; – I say, I come
From your good queen.

LEONTES   Good queen!

PAULINA   Good queen, my lord, good queen: I say good
     queen,
And would by combat make her good, so were I   60
A man, the worst about you.

LEONTES   Force her hence.

PAULINA   Let him that makes but trifles of his eyes
First hand me: on mine own accord I'll off;
But first, I'll do my errand. The good queen
(For she is good) hath brought you forth a
     daughter;   65
Here 'tis; [*Laying down the* BABY] commends it to
     your blessing.

LEONTES   Out!
A mankind witch! Hence with her, out o' door:
A most intelligencing bawd!

PAULINA   Not so:
I am as ignorant in that, as you
In so entitling me: and no less honest   70
Than you are mad; which is enough, I'll warrant,
As the world goes, to pass for honest.

LEONTES   Traitors!
Will you not push her out? Give her the bastard,
Thou dotard! thou art woman-tired, unroosted
By thy dame Partlet here. Take up the bastard,   75
Take 't up, I say; give 't to thy crone.

Leontes is helpless before Paulina's onslaught and her tacit
support from his courtiers. He can only abuse her and her
husband. She describes Leontes as a traitor to himself and
claims to see in the baby a physical likeness to the king.

77 **Unvenerable**: dishonoured; literally, unsaintly

78 **forced baseness**: name of bastard inflicted upon it

86–90 **and will not...sound**: he will not (and since he is the
king shamefully he cannot be compelled to) change his
opinion. The root of his opinion is as rotten as the strong
things are sound.

90 **callat**: a lewd woman, a shrew, a scold

91 **beat**: Jacobean pronunciation is likely to have emphasized
the angry pun on baits in the next line

92 **baits**: torments

94 **dam**: mother – see Act 1 scene 2 line 137 and note on
page 14

96–97 **might we lay...worse**: we might charge you with
fulfilling the old proverb that 'the child is so like you it is
worse'

98–99 **print, matter And copy**: literally font size, content and
wording, the metaphor being taken from printing. Paulina
praises Leontes as the author of his daughter.

100 **trick**: characteristic expression
valley: between nose and upper lip or, perhaps, the cleft in
the chin

102 **mould and frame**: again words which emphasize Leontes
the maker

- *What is the mood and tone of the scene now? How is the
audience likely to react to Paulina's tirade?*

PAULINA   [*To* ANTIGONUS] For ever
              Unvenerable be thy hands, if thou
              Tak'st up the princess, by that forced baseness
              Which he has put upon 't!

LEONTES   He dreads his wife.

PAULINA   So I would you did; then 'twere past all doubt   80
              You'd call your children yours.

LEONTES   A nest of traitors!

ANTIGONUS   I am none, by this good light.

PAULINA   Nor I; nor any
              But one that's here, and that's himself; for he,
              The sacred honour of himself, his queen's,
              His hopeful son's, his babe's, betrays to slander,   85
              Whose sting is sharper than the sword's; and will
                  not
              (For, as the case now stands, it is a curse
              He cannot be compelled to 't) once remove
              The root of his opinion, which is rotten
              As ever oak or stone was sound.

LEONTES   A callat   90
              Of boundless tongue, who late hath beat her
                  husband,
              And now baits me! This brat is none of mine;
              It is the issue of Polixenes.
              Hence with it, and together with the dam
              Commit them to the fire!

PAULINA   It is yours;   95
              And, might we lay th' old proverb to your charge,
              So like you, 'tis the worse. Behold, my lords,
              Although the print be little, the whole matter
              And copy of the father: eye, nose, lip;
              The trick of's frown; his forehead; nay, the
                  valley,   100
              The pretty dimples of his chin and cheek; his smiles;
              The very mould and frame of hand, nail, finger:
              And thou, good goddess Nature, which hast made

The impasse continues. Paulina charges Leontes with being tyrant. She is gradually forced from the room but still seems to get the last word.

104 got: begot; fathered

106 yellow: the colour of gall and thus associated with jealousy

107 not: are not. Since Paulina suggests that the child might not know the father of her own children it is clear that she is continuing in sarcastic mode.

108 lozel: worthless fellow: said to Antigonus

114–115 It is an....in 't: it is the beliefs and behaviour of the woman who burns in the fire that makes it a just punishment (or otherwise), not merely that the sentence is carried out. There is also a suggestion that it is Leontes who is the heretic in failing to believe Hermione's faithfulness. The implication that, in either case, the sentence could be unjust leads naturally into Paulina's suggestion of tyranny which follows.

118 weak-hinged fancy: barely-supported imaginings
something savours: has the stench

120 On your allegiance: on your oaths of loyalty to me

121–122 Were I...life?: if I were a tyrant why haven't I already had her killed?

126 A better guiding spirit: Paulina may be implying either herself or Leontes, and perhaps both of them
What needs these hands?: Keep your hands off me!

127 You, that...follies: you (courtiers) that treat his madness with such gentleness

> • *Who is getting the better of these exchanges? How? What movements and stage business might accompany them?*

	So like to him that got it, if thou hast	
	The ordering of the mind too, 'mongst all	
	colours	105
	No yellow in 't, lest she suspect, as he does,	
	Her children not her husband's!	

LEONTES   A gross hag!
And, lozel, thou art worthy to be hanged,
That wilt not stay her tongue.

ANTIGONUS   Hang all the husbands
That cannot do that feat, you'll leave yourself   110
Hardly one subject.

LEONTES   Once more, take her hence.

PAULINA   A most unworthy and unnatural lord
Can do no more.

LEONTES   I'll ha' thee burnt.

PAULINA   I care not:
It is an heretic that makes the fire,
Not she which burns in 't. I'll not call you
     tyrant;   115
But this most cruel usage of your queen –
Not able to produce more accusation
Than your own weak-hinged fancy – something
     savours
Of tyranny, and will ignoble make you,
Yea, scandalous to the world.

LEONTES   On your allegiance,   120
Out of the chamber with her! Were I a tyrant,
Where were her life? she durst not call me so,
If she did know me one. Away with her!

PAULINA   I pray you, do not push me; I'll be gone.
Look at your babe, my lord: 'tis yours: Jove send
     her   125
A better guiding spirit! What needs these
     hands?
You, that are thus so tender o'er his follies,

Paulina exits but leaves the baby behind. Leontes blames Antigonus for his wife's intervention and commands him to have the child destroyed by fire. A Lord speaks up for Antigonus and intercedes for the baby. Leontes cannot decide what to do.

136 by good testimony: confirmed by reliable witnesses
137 With what...thine: with all the rest of your possessions
139 these my proper hands: my own hands. The emphasis provided by the apparently superfluous 'proper' not only underlines the horror of the act but suggests that Leontes, referring to other uses of the word, thinks it lawful and appropriate.
146 give us better credit: believe better of us
147 beseech': beseech you
157 You sir: said to Antigonus
158 tenderly officious: so kind in the office of husband
159 Margery: hen (slang), used sarcastically as is 'midwife': compare line 75 above

> • *What is the evidence here for Leontes' instability, moral weakness and consequent lack of authority?*

	Will never do him good, not one of you.	
	So, so: farewell; we are gone.	[*Exit*
LEONTES	Thou, traitor, hast set on thy wife to this.	130
	My child? Away with 't! Even thou, that hast	
	A heart so tender o'er it, take it hence	
	And see it instantly consumed with fire;	
	Even thou, and none but thou. Take it up straight:	
	Within this hour bring me word 'tis done,	135
	And by good testimony, or I'll seize thy life,	
	With what thou else call'st thine. If thou refuse	
	And wilt encounter with my wrath, say so;	
	The bastard brains with these my proper hands	
	Shall I dash out. Go, take it to the fire;	140
	For thou set'st on thy wife.	
ANTIGONUS	I did not, sir:	
	These lords, my noble fellows, if they please,	
	Can clear me in 't.	
LORDS	We can: my royal liege,	
	He is not guilty of her coming hither.	
LEONTES	You're liars all.	145
A LORD	Beseech your highness, give us better credit:	
	We have always truly served you; and beseech'	
	So to esteem of us: and on our knees we beg	
	(As recompense of our dear services	
	Past and to come) that you do change this	
	purpose,	150
	Which being so horrible, so bloody, must	
	Lead on to some foul issue. We all kneel.	
LEONTES	I am a feather for each wind that blows:	
	Shall I live on to see this bastard kneel	
	And call me father? Better burn it now	155
	Than curse it then. But be it: let it live.	
	It shall not neither. You sir, come you hither,	
	You that have been so tenderly officious	
	With Lady Margery, your midwife there,	
	To save this bastard's life – for 'tis a bastard,	160

Leontes tells Antigonus that the only way to save the lives of himself, his wife and the baby is for him to take the child to some foreign wilderness and there to leave it exposed to the elements. Antigonus reluctantly agrees.

161 **this beard's grey**: if Leontes is only in his early thirties (see Act 1 scene 2 line 155) then the beard probably belongs to Antigonus who is much older (see below line 165 and Act 5 scene 3)

   adventure: risk

163 **That my ability may undergo**: that my abilities will allow me to perform successfully

164 **And nobleness impose**: Antigonus appeals to Leontes' nobility in the hope that he will not set a task that could dishonour either of them

165 **pawn**: pledge; place in your safe keeping

169 **fail**: failure

171 **lewd-tongued**: rude, vulgar. See 'callat', line 90 above, and note.

174 **This female bastard**: compare lines 75–81

177 **it**: an old form of the possessive pronoun 'its'

178, 181 **strange, strangely**: Leontes puns on the word which could mean foreign – as was Polixenes.

183 **present**: immediate

185 **kites and ravens**: scavenging birds, though Antigonus may be remembering that ravens were commanded to feed the Old Testament prophet Elijah (1 Kings 17.4)

189 **In more...require**: more than is justified by this deed

190 **thy**: referring to the baby

191 **loss**: destruction

- *Why does Leontes give way to the entreaties of his courtiers? What is the dramatic significance of this change of mind?*

So sure as this beard's grey – what will you
    adventure
To save this brat's life?

ANTIGONUS   Anything, my lord,
That my ability may undergo,
And nobleness impose: at least thus much –
I'll pawn the little blood which I have left   165
To save the innocent: anything possible.

LEONTES   It shall be possible. Swear by this sword
Thou wilt perform my bidding.

ANTIGONUS   I will, my lord.

LEONTES   Mark and perform it: seest thou? For the fail
Of any point in 't shall not only be   170
Death to thyself, but to thy lewd-tongued wife
(Whom for this time we pardon). We enjoin thee,
As thou art liege-man to us, that thou carry
This female bastard hence, and that thou bear it
To some remote and desert place, quite out   175
Of our dominions; and that there thou leave it
(Without more mercy) to it own protection
And favour of the climate. As by strange fortune
It came to us, I do in justice charge thee,
On thy soul's peril and thy body's torture,   180
That thou commend it strangely to some place
Where chance may nurse or end it. Take it up.

ANTIGONUS   I swear to do this; though a present death
Had been more merciful. Come on, poor babe:
Some powerful spirit instruct the kites and
    ravens   185
To be thy nurses! Wolves and bears,they say,
Casting their savageness aside, have done
Like offices of pity. Sir, be prosperous
In more than this deed does require; and blessing
Against this cruelty, fight on thy side,   190
Poor thing, condemned to loss!

                              [*Exit with the* BABY

As Antigonus leaves with the baby, Leontes tries again to justify his behaviour. A servant announces the return of Cleomenes and Dion with the message from the Oracle of Apollo. Leontes commands Hermione be brought to public trial.

199 **suddenly**: very quickly
201 **Summon a session...arraign**: convene a court of justice so that I may formally accuse

LEONTES   No: I'll not rear
            Another's issue.

            Enter a SERVANT

SERVANT   Please your highness, posts
            From those you sent to th' Oracle, are come
            An hour since: Cleomenes and Dion,
            Being well arrived from Delphos, are both
                landed,   195
            Hasting to th' court.

A LORD   So please you, sir, their speed
            Hath been beyond account.

LEONTES   Twenty-three days
            They have been absent: 'tis good speed; foretells
            The great Apollo suddenly will have
            The truth of this appear. Prepare you, lords;   200
            Summon a session, that we may arraign
            Our most disloyal lady; for, as she hath
            Been publicly accused, so shall she have
            A just and open trial. While she lives
            My heart will be a burden to me. Leave me.   205
            And think upon my bidding.   [*Exeunt severally*

Keeping track

Scene 1

1 In which lines do we learn of Hermione's pregnancy?
2 What does the departure of Camillo and Polixenes prove to Leontes?
3 How does he now respond to his son, Mamillius?
4 Describe the way that Leontes speaks about his wife to the courtiers.
5 How does Hermione react to his public accusations?
6 What is the reaction of the courtiers to what has happened?
7 What are the reasons for Leontes' decision to consult the Oracle?

Scene 2

1 What news is given to Paulina by Emilia?
2 What does Paulina decide to do?
3 Does Emilia agree wholeheartedly with Paulina's plan?
4 How does Paulina persuade the Gaoler that he should let her take the baby away from the prison?

Scene 3

1 At the beginning of the scene, how – according to Leontes – can he achieve some peace of mind?
2 What do we learn about the state of health of Mamillius? What explanations does Leontes give for this?
3 What reasons does Paulina give for coming to see the king?
4 How does Leontes respond to Paulina?
5 What does the king ask Antigonus to do? Why is Antigonus given this responsibility?
6 Why is Leontes determined to have 'a just and open trial'?

Characters

Hermione

1 What is shown of Hermione's relationship with her son? Why is it important that we are shown this? What is the dramatic impact of their scene together?
2 After Leontes accuses her of being 'an adult'ress' in scene 1, how does Hermione respond?
3 In her last speech in scene 1 (lines 116–124), how does Hermione take control of the situation?
4 What new qualities do you observe in Hermione in this act?

Leontes

During this act other characters often disagree with Leontes or fail to carry out his commands.

1 List examples of disobedience or disagreement.
2 How does the king respond when his courtiers disagree with him?
3 What do the reactions of other people show us about him and the way he behaves?
4 How does his soliloquy at the beginning of scene 3 (lines 1–26) affect our attitude towards him? (The CLOSE STUDY section below gives you an opportunity to study this speech in more detail.)

Paulina

1 Paulina seems to be totally without fear:
   '*Let him that makes but trifles of his eyes*
   First hand me' (scene 3 lines 62–63).
   What other qualities does she exhibit in Act 2? Find a quotation or example of her behaviour to illustrate each quality.
2 How is she like Camillo and in what sense has she taken over his role in the court of Sicilia?

Themes

1 Leontes' rash behaviour is increasingly being contrasted by the *integrity* of other characters. Make a list of characters whose behaviour is honest, truthful, noble or shows integrity in any way.
2 Here as in many other plays Shakespeare explores the nature of *authority* and *kingship*. In what ways does Leontes demonstrate that he is a king? In what ways does he show a lack of authority? What limits do there seem to be to Leontes' power?

Drama

1 Use FORUM THEATRE techniques (see page 263) to explore one or more of the following moments of high tension:
   • scene 1 line 56 – '*Give me the boy...*'
   • scene 1 line 115 – '*Shall I be heard...*'
   • scene 3 line 58 – '*Good queen!*'
   • scene 3 line 92 – '*This brat is none of mine...*'.
2 Work in groups of four. Imagine two of your group are newspaper reporters who are interviewing one of the courtiers and one of the servants present during the events of scene 3. Remember that it may not be possible to recount all that has happened without being guilty of treason. (This activity could be linked to number 2 in the WRITING section below.)

3 • Learn the 'spider' speech (scene 1 lines 36–52).
   • In groups of seven or eight (or as a whole class) create a still image
     of the royal court surrounding Leontes at the moment of this
     soliloquy. Take turns to portray Leontes. He goes from one person
     to another in the still image saying a sentence to each. Try to use
     the words in a variety of ways. For example: you could run from
     one to the next, or you could grab each person and try to convince
     them of what you are saying.

Close study

Act 2 scene 3 lines 1–26

This section is essentially a soliloquy, interrupted first by the servant and
then by Paulina. Consuming jealousy has given way to a desire for
vengeance.

1 Summarize Leontes' thoughts about Hermione.
2 What does he decide to do about her and Polixenes?
3 Leontes is briefly concerned about Mamillius' sickness. What other
   concerns push his son from his mind?
4 Does he use any imagery which was characteristic of his speech in
   Act 1?
5 What mistakes and misjudgements of other people does Leontes
   reveal here?

Key scene

Scene 3 lines 26–192

Keying it in

1 First go back to scene 1 lines 36–52.
   • What did that speech show us of Leontes' state of mind?
   • How has his thinking developed since?
2 Now look at scene 1 lines 172–199.
   • How does Leontes justify the guilt of Polixenes and Hermione?
   • He says that he does not need further confirmation of his own
     knowledge. Why, then, does he send Cleomenes and Dion to the
     Oracle? What does this reveal about his control of the situation?
   • What do the last two lines of scene 1 reveal about the attitude of
     Antigonus and the court in general?

The scene itself

3 Lines 26–39
   • How does Paulina persuade the Lords that she should be allowed in?
   • Look particularly at the images of sleep, rest and medicine. In what

ways does Paulina demonstrate the unreality of the world which
Leontes has created for himself and in which his courtiers collude?

4 Lines 46–52
- What is Paulina's tone of voice?
- How is her strength of character shown?
- How would you describe her relationship with her husband?

5 Lines 53–129
Consider the ways that Paulina presents her case to Leontes.
- How does her language stress the innocence of Hermione?
- How does she show her strength of character?
- How does she use the baby to appeal to Leontes' better nature?
- How does she retain her dignity and composure?
- Why does she leave the child behind?
- How do Leontes' responses to Paulina show his inability to listen to
  reason and the narrowness of his mind?

6 Lines 130–162
- What are Leontes' intentions?
- What is his opinion of Antigonus, Paulina and their relationship?

7 Lines 162–192
- What qualities does Antigonus reveal in this section? Use quotation
  as evidence for your judgement.

Overview

8 Leontes says '*I am a feather for each wind that blows*' (line 153). What
evidence of this do you find within the scene?

Writing

1 After Hermione has been taken away to prison she reflects on what has
happened. Write her monologue.
2 (This can be linked to activity 2 in the DRAMA section above.) Write
the newspaper report of the events of scene 3 following your interview
with one of the courtiers and one of the servants who were present.
You could ask another member of your group to act as editor and
censor, putting a thin line through anything that is either inaccurate or
unpublishable.
3 Paulina and Antigonus have high standards of integrity. What do they
do which is evidence for this? What methods do they use in order to
combat Leontes' tyranny? Do you think they are justified?
4 What are the characteristics of Leontes' behaviour as a king? What
does this act show us about the extent of his power and his authority?
How does his behaviour compare with what we know of Polixenes?

A flashback. Cleomenes and Dion are on their return journey from Delphos. They describe the beauty of the island and the spiritual experience they had there. They believe the sealed prophecy of the Oracle will reveal something extraordinary.

1 **delicate**: delightful
2 **the isle**: Delphos; see Act 2 scene 1 line 183 and note
4 **caught**: struck
    celestial habits: heavenly robes – with a pun on both words
6 **grave wearers**: respected and serious wearers of the 'celestial habits'
8 **the burst**: the thundering voice
11 **th' event**: outcome
12 **O be 't so!**: oh let it be so; as I fervently hope it will be
13 **rare**: excellent
14 **This time...on 't**: the time has been well spent on it
16 **forcing**: unjustly thrusting
17 **carriage**: conduct
18 **clear or end**: bring to a good or bad conclusion (compare Act 2 scene 3 line 182)
19 **Thus by...sealed up**: thus sealed by the High Priest of Apollo. Dion and Cleomenes are apparently carrying a sealed document or casket.
20 **discover**: reveal
    rare: extraordinary
21 **Even then...knowledge**: will immediately become public knowledge

> • *This scene heralds a change of mood. What details of description and language are used to effect this?*

Act three

Scene 1

Enter CLEOMENES *and* DION

CLEOMENES The climate's delicate, the air most sweet,
Fertile the isle, the temple much surpassing
The common praise it bears.

DION   I shall report,
For most it caught me, the celestial habits
(Methinks I so should term them), and the
    reverence   5
Of the grave wearers. O, the sacrifice!
How ceremonious, solemn and unearthly
It was i' th' off'ring!

CLEOMENES   But of all, the burst
And the ear-deaf'ning voice o' th' Oracle,
Kin to Jove's thunder, so surprised my sense,   10
That I was nothing.

DION   If th' event o' th' journey
Prove as successful to the queen, – O be 't so! –
As it hath been to us, rare, pleasant, speedy,
This time is worth the use on 't.

CLEOMENES   Great Apollo
Turn all to th' best! These proclamations,   15
So forcing faults upon Hermione,
I little like.

DION   The violent carriage of it
Will clear or end the business: when the Oracle
(Thus by Apollo's great divine sealed up)
Shall the contents discover, something rare   20
Even then will rush to knowledge. Go: fresh horses!
And gracious be the issue.   [*Exeunt*

The trial of Hermione. Leontes clears himself of the charge of being tyrannous by holding the trial in public. Hermione is brought in and the charge of treason, adultery and conspiracy is read. She claims that, since she is unable to call witnesses in her support, there is little point in her 'not guilty' plea.

1 **sessions**: court of justice (see Act 2 scene 3 lines 201–204)
2 **Even pushes...heart**: strikes at my heart – since it threatens Hermione, whom he loves, but is concerned with treason which threatens his monarchy. The ambiguity is emphasized by the word 'even'.
4 **Of us...beloved**: loved too much by me
5 **tyrannous**: compare Act 2 scene 3 lines 115–123
6 **which shall have due course**: which shall proceed through the appropriate legal process
7 **purgation**: acquittal; in earlier times the word described the process of establishing innocence through a judicial ordeal
13 **arraigned**: called upon to answer the charge of
17 **pretence**: plot
22 **but**: only
24–25 **The testimony...myself**: I have no witness to support me other than what I can say in my own defence
25 **scarce boot**: hardly help
26–28 **mine integrity...received**: when I act honestly my actions are considered treason, so my words of justification are sure to be accounted lies

> • *Another change of mood. What mood is being established and how might the staging of this scene emphasize the contrast with the previous scene?*

Scene 2

Enter LEONTES, LORDS *and* OFFICERS

LEONTES   This sessions (to our great grief we pronounce)
           Even pushes 'gainst our heart: the party tried
           The daughter of a king, our wife, and one
           Of us too much beloved. Let us be cleared
           Of being tyrannous, since we so openly   5
           Proceed in justice, which shall have due course,
           Even to the guilt or the purgation.
           Produce the prisoner.

OFFICER   It is his highness' pleasure that the queen
           Appear in person, here in court. Silence!   10

Enter HERMIONE, *guarded;* PAULINA *and* LADIES
attending

LEONTES   Read the indictment.

OFFICER   [*Reads*] Hermione, queen to the worthy Leontes,
           king of Sicilia, thou art here accused and arraigned
           of high treason, in committing adultery with
           Polixenes, King of Bohemia, and conspiring   15
           with Camillo to take away the life of our sovereign
           lord the King, thy royal husband: the pretence
           whereof being by circumstances partly laid open,
           thou, Hermione, contrary to the faith and
           allegiance of a true subject, didst counsel and   20
           aid them, for their better safety, to fly away by night.

HERMIONE   Since what I am to say, must be but that
           Which contradicts my accusation, and
           The testimony on my part, no other
           But what comes from myself, it shall scarce
                                              boot me   25
           To say 'not guilty': mine integrity,
           Being counted falsehood, shall, as I express it,

Hermione places her faith in the gods who, she says, know her innocence. She reminds Leontes of her chastity and the honour in which she is held as the wife and daughter of a king. Her honour is, she says, her children's most important inheritance. Leontes disputes with her.

28 But thus: however

34 continent: controlled, especially in respect of sexual behaviour

35–37 more Than...spectators: more unhappy than anyone else (real or imagined), even than any character in a play devised to move an audience

38 owe: own

39 A moiety: half

41 prate: talk to no purpose

41–42 'fore Who please: before whoever it pleases

42–43 For life...spare: I value life in the same way that I would grief – I would spare my life and spare myself grief

43–45 for honour...stand for: as for my honour, it is my children's inheritance and the only thing I fight for here

49–50 With what...thus: with what improper relationship I have overstepped the mark that I should appear here in court

50–51 one jot...bound: the smallest amount beyond the limit

51 or, or: either, or

54 fie: shame

55–57 wanted Less...first: had less impudence in self-justification than was needed to perform the sin in the first place. Leontes is sarcastic and uses the double negative for emphasis in this speech.

58 due: appropriate

59 own: acknowledge. Leontes responds to Hermione's use of 'due'.

59–61 More than...acknowledge: I do not acknowledge any fault as mine except that which is now being called a fault (her honourable friendship with Polixenes which she justifies in the following lines)

> • *What features of Hermione's speech make her sound honest and persuasive?*

Be so received. But thus, if powers divine
Behold our human actions (as they do),
I doubt not then but innocence shall make   30
False accusation blush, and tyranny
Tremble at patience. You, my lord, best know
(Who least will seem to do so) my past life
Hath been as continent, as chaste, as true,
As I am now unhappy; which is more   35
Than history can pattern, though devised
And played to take spectators. For behold me,
A fellow of the royal bed, which owe
A moiety of the throne, a great king's daughter,
The mother to a hopeful prince, here standing   40
To prate and talk for life and honour 'fore
Who please to come and hear. For life, I prize it
As I weigh grief (which I would spare): for honour,
'Tis a derivative from me to mine,
And only that I stand for. I appeal   45
To your own conscience, sir, before Polixenes
Came to your court, how I was in your grace,
How merited to be so; since he came,
With what encounter so uncurrent I
Have strained t'appear thus: if one jot beyond   50
The bound of honour, or in act or will
That way inclining, hardened be the hearts
Of all that hear me, and my near'st of kin
Cry 'fie' upon my grave!

LEONTES   I ne'er heard yet
That any of these bolder vices wanted   55
Less impudence to gainsay what they did
Than to perform it first.

HERMIONE   That's true enough,
Though 'tis a saying, sir, not due to me.

LEONTES   You will not own it.

HERMIONE   More than mistress of

Hermione defends her relationship with Polixenes, and Camillo's honesty. She accuses Leontes of imagining treason. He threatens her with torture and death.

64 become: be appropriate to

72–73 though it be...how: even though it may have been served up to me and I persuaded to try it

76 Wotting: if they know

81–82 My life...down: my life, which I will lay down, is the target of your imagination (compare Act 2 scene 3 lines 5–6)

85 of your fact: who do evil deeds like you

86 concerns more than avails: is troublesome rather than helpful to you

87 like to itself: as an illegitimate child should be

90–91 in whose...death: the most merciful outcome of the sentence you should expect is death. This is a repetition of the threat to burn Hermione and, perhaps, a suggestion of further torture.

	Which comes to me in the name of fault, I must	
	not	60
	At all acknowledge. For Polixenes,	
	With whom I am accused, I do confess	
	I loved him as in honour he required,	
	With such a kind of love as might become	
	A lady like me; with a love, even such,	65
	So, and no other, as yourself commanded:	
	Which, not to have done, I think had been in me	
	Both disobedience and ingratitude	
	To you, and toward your friend, whose love had	
	spoke,	
	Even since it could speak, from an infant, freely,	70
	That it was yours. Now, for conspiracy,	
	I know not how it tastes, though it be dished	
	For me to try how: all I know of it,	
	Is that Camillo was an honest man;	
	And why he left your court, the gods themselves	75
	(Wotting no more than I) are ignorant.	

LEONTES   You knew of his departure, as you know
           What you have underta'en to do in 's absence.

HERMIONE   Sir,
           You speak a language that I understand not: 80
           My life stands in the level of your dreams,
           Which I'll lay down.

LEONTES   Your actions are my dreams.
           You had a bastard by Polixenes,
           And I but dreamed it! As you were past all shame
           (Those of your fact are so) so past all truth,   85
           Which to deny, concerns more than avails; for as
           Thy brat hath been cast out, like to itself,
           No father owning it (which is, indeed,
           More criminal in thee than it), so thou
           Shalt feel our justice; in whose easiest passage   90
           Look for no less than death.

HERMIONE   Sir, spare your threats:

Hermione says that since she has been deprived of her husband, her children and her reputation, and since she has been physically abused, she no longer fears to die. She would, however, preserve her honour and calls upon the Oracle to vindicate her. Cleomenes and Dion are brought in.

92 bug: terrible spirit (from the Welsh *bwg* meaning ghost, which also gives us bugbear and bogey)

93 no commodity: of no profit or value

97 his: that is, Mamillius

99 Starred most unluckily: born under an unlucky conjunction of stars (compare Act 1 scene 2 line 202 and Act 2 scene 1 line 105)

101 Haled: hauled violently
    post: the post outside a sheriff's house on which official public notices were fixed

102 strumpet: prostitute

103 child-bed privilege: the prescribed period of rest after childbirth
    'longs: belongs

106 strength of limit: strength gained through the 'child-bed privilege' – see line 103 above

111 free: that is, from slander. Compare lines 42–45 above.

112 surmises: unproved allegations

112–113 else But what: other than those which

114 rigour: harshness

122 flatness: completeness

The bug which you would fright me with, I seek.
To me can life be no commodity;
The crown and comfort of my life, your favour,
I do give lost, for I do feel it gone,   95
But know not how it went. My second joy,
And first-fruits of my body, from his presence
I am barred, like one infectious. My third comfort
(Starred most unluckily) is from my breast
(The innocent milk in it most innocent mouth)   100
Haled out to murder; myself on every post
Proclaimed a strumpet, with immodest hatred
The child-bed privilege denied, which 'longs
To women of all fashion; lastly, hurried
Here, to this place, i' th' open air, before   105
I have got strength of limit. Now, my liege,
Tell me what blessings I have here alive,
That I should fear to die? Therefore proceed.
But yet hear this: mistake me not: no life,
I prize it not a straw, but for mine honour,   110
Which I would free: if I shall be condemned
Upon surmises, all proofs sleeping else
But what your jealousies awake, I tell you
'Tis rigour and not law. Your honours all,
I do refer me to the Oracle: 115
Apollo be my judge!

A LORD   This your request
Is altogether just: therefore bring forth,
And in Apollo's name, his Oracle.

                         [*Exeunt certain* OFFICERS

HERMIONE   The Emperor of Russia was my father:
O that he were alive, and here beholding   120
His daughter's trial! That he did but see
The flatness of my misery, yet with eyes
Of pity, not revenge!

          Enter OFFICERS *with* CLEOMENES *and* DION

OFFICER   You here shall swear upon this sword of justice,

Cleomenes and Dion take the oath. The Oracle is read but
Leontes refuses to believe it. Immediately a servant enters to
announce the death of Mamillius. Leontes realizes that the
Oracle is indeed true. Hermione collapses.

140 i' th': in the
144–145 mere conceit...speed: imagining and fearing for the
     queen's fate

• *Hermione's rhetoric gives way to simple expression and
rapid action. How is the drama of this scene
generated? What events will involve members of the
audience and what rapidly changing emotions are
they likely to experience?*

	That you, Cleomenes and Dion, have	125
	Been both at Delphos, and from thence have brought	
	This sealed-up Oracle, by the hand delivered	
	Of great Apollo's priest; and that since then	
	You have not dared to break the holy seal,	
	Nor read the secrets in 't.	

CLEOMENES
DION   }   All this we swear.   130

LEONTES   Break up the seals and read.

OFFICER   [*Reads*] Hermione is chaste; Polixenes blameless;
          Camillo a true subject; Leontes a jealous tyrant; his
          innocent babe truly begotten; and the king shall
          live without an heir if that which is lost be not   135
          found.

LORDS   Now blessed be the great Apollo!

HERMIONE   Praised!

LEONTES   Hast thou read truth?

OFFICER   Ay, my lord, even so
          As it is here set down.

LEONTES   There is no truth at all i' th' Oracle: 140
          The sessions shall proceed: this is mere falsehood.

          Enter SERVANT

SERVANT   My lord the king, the king!

LEONTES   What is the business?

SERVANT   O sir, I shall be hated to report it!
          The prince your son, with mere conceit and fear
          Of the queen's speed, is gone.

LEONTES   How! gone?

SERVANT   Is dead.   145

LEONTES   Apollo's angry, and the heavens themselves
          Do strike at my injustice. [HERMIONE *faints*] How
          now there?

Paulina reports that Hermione is dying: Leontes instructs
her to remove the queen and care for her. He asks Apollo for
forgiveness and promises to put right all his errors. He
reveals how he had attempted to corrupt Camillo and praises
his honour. Paulina returns, apparently in great distress.

148 is mortal to: kills
150 but o'ercharged: only over-burdened
160 minister: Leontes plays on Camillo's role as his minister and
    in administering the poison
161 had: would have
162 tardied: delayed
163–165 though I with...done: I threatened him with death if
    he did not do the deed but encouraged him by promising a
    reward if it were done
167 Unclasped my practice: disclosed my plot
168 certain: this word is omitted from the *First Folio* but the
    correction which is made in the *Second Folio* improves the
    metre and balances 'incertainties' in the next line.
170 No richer than his honour: his honour was his entire
    wealth
    glisters: sparkles
171 Thorough: through
172 Woe the while!: Alas for this moment!
173 cut my lace: that is, of her stays or tightly-fitting bodice
175 studied torments: premeditated tortures. A list follows.

> • *What does Leontes reveal here that will not be known to*
> *his courtiers?*

PAULINA   This news is mortal to the queen: look down
               And see what death is doing.

LEONTES   Take her hence:
               Her heart is but o'ercharged: she will recover.   150
               I have too much believed mine own suspicion:
               Beseech you, tenderly apply to her
               Some remedies for life.
                       [*Exeunt* PAULINA *and* LADIES, *with* HERMIONE
                                   Apollo, pardon
               My great profaneness 'gainst thine Oracle!
               I'll reconcile me to Polixenes,   155
               New woo my queen, recall the good Camillo,
               Whom I proclaim a man of truth, of mercy:
               For being transported by my jealousies
               To bloody thoughts and to revenge, I chose
               Camillo for the minister to poison   160
               My friend Polixenes: which had been done,
               But that the good mind of Camillo tardied
               My swift command; though I with death, and with
               Reward, did threaten and encourage him,
               Not doing it, and being done. He (most
                   humane   165
               And filled with honour) to my kingly guest
               Unclasped my practice, quit his fortunes here
               (Which you knew great) and to the certain hazard
               Of all incertainties, himself commended,
               No richer than his honour: how he glisters   170
               Thorough my rust! and how his piety
               Does my deeds make the blacker!

               Enter PAULINA

PAULINA   Woe the while!
               O cut my lace, lest my heart, cracking it,
               Break too!

A LORD   What fit is this, good lady?

PAULINA   What studied torments, tyrant, hast for me?   175

Paulina launches a savage verbal attack upon Leontes, chronicling his mistakes and misdeeds and culminating in the revelation that Hermione is dead.

176 wheels: victims were spreadeagled on a large wheel which provided the frame for further tortures
racks: frames with a roller at each end. A person was attached by the wrists and ankles and the rollers turned in order to stretch the joints. This crippling apparatus was in use in the Tower of London during Shakespeare's lifetime.
flaying: to strip the skin from a living body
177 leads: molten lead
178 whose: I whose
181 Fancies...idle: imaginings too foolish for boys, too childish and silly
184 spices: foretastes
186 of a fool: fool that you are
188–189 Thou would'st...king: close reading of the text would suggest that it is not possible for Paulina to know this detail since she had left the stage with Hermione during Leontes' confession, but the audience knows and, in the theatre, is more likely to react to the dramatic effect of her diatribe than to perceive the inconsistency
189–90 poor trespasses...by: but these are little sins compared with those which followed
193 shed water out of fire: shed tears amongst the fires of hell or from his flaming eyes
197 conceive: comprehend that
200 said: spoken of it
202 higher powers: gods
205 Tincture or...eye: colour to her lips or a sparkle to her eyes
206 Heat outwardly: warmth to her body

- *What features of Paulina's speech make it exciting and dramatic?*

What wheels, racks, fires? What flaying, boiling,
In leads or oils? What old or newer torture
Must I receive, whose every word deserves
To taste of thy most worst? Thy tyranny,
Together working with thy jealousies   180
(Fancies too weak for boys, too green and idle
For girls of nine), O think what they have done,
And then run mad indeed: stark mad! for all
Thy by-gone fooleries were but spices of it.
That thou betray'dst Polixenes, 'twas nothing;   185
That did but show thee, of a fool, inconstant
And damnable ingrateful: nor was't much,
Thou would'st have poisoned good Camillo's
    honour,
To have him kill a king; poor trespasses,
Most monstrous standing by: whereof I reckon 190
The casting forth to crows thy baby daughter,
To be or none or little; though a devil
Would have shed water out of fire, ere done 't:
Nor is't directly laid to thee the death
Of the young prince, whose honourable
    thoughts   195
(Thoughts high for one so tender) cleft the heart
That could conceive a gross and foolish sire
Blemished his gracious dam: this is not, no,
Laid to thy answer. But the last – O lords,
When I have said, cry 'woe!' – the queen, the
    queen,   200
The sweet'st dear'st creature's dead: and vengeance
    for 't
Not dropped down yet.

A LORD   The higher powers forbid!

PAULINA   I say she's dead: I'll swear 't. If word nor oath
Prevail not, go and see. If you can bring
Tincture or lustre in her lip, her eye,   205
Heat outwardly or breath within, I'll serve you
As I would do the gods. But, O thou tyrant!

Paulina tells Leontes that no penitence can match the
enormity of his sin. Leontes is distraught. Paulina apologizes
but continues to remind the king of all that he has
destroyed. Leontes prepares to bury his wife and son. He
pledges to erect a monument to them.

208–209 heavier Than all thy woes can stir: greater than any
act of penitence can change
210 A thousand knees: a thousand people at prayer upon their
knees. Paulina uses synecdoche, a rhetorical figure of speech
in which a part represents the whole in order to create a
more vivid description.
212 still: always
214 that way thou wert: towards you (as a sign that you are
forgiven)
223 Should be past grief: should not be grieved for
223–224 Do not receive...petition: do not be troubled by my
prayers for vengeance
225 minded: reminded
226 good my liege: my good lord and king
230 remember: remind
231 take your patience to you: rely upon your patience
233–234 which I receive...thee: I accept the truth of what you
say and therefore do not need your pity
236 them: that is, the gravestones

- *What is the tone, or tones, of Paulina's words to Leontes
  on this page? How convincing is the change of mood
  and behaviour by both Leontes and Paulina?*

Do not repent these things, for they are heavier
Than all thy woes can stir: therefore betake thee
To nothing but despair. A thousand knees   210
Ten thousand years together, naked, fasting,
Upon a barren mountain, and still winter
In storm perpetual, could not move the gods
To look that way thou wert.

LEONTES   Go on, go on:
Thou canst not speak too much. I have
    deserved   215
All tongues to talk their bitt'rest.

A LORD   [*To* PAULINA] Say no more:
Howe'er the business goes, you have made fault
I' th' boldness of your speech.

PAULINA   I am sorry for 't:
All faults I make, when I shall come to know them,
I do repent. Alas! I have showed too much   220
The rashness of a woman: he is touched
To th' noble heart. What's gone and what's past
    help
Should be past grief. Do not receive affliction
At my petition; I beseech you, rather
Let me be punished, that have minded you   225
Of what you should forget. Now, good my liege,
Sir, royal sir, forgive a foolish woman:
The love I bore your queen – lo, fool again!
I'll speak of her no more, nor of your children:
I'll not remember you of my own lord   230
(Who is lost too): take your patience to you,
And I'll say nothing.

LEONTES   Thou didst speak but well
When most the truth: which I receive much better
Than to be pitied of thee. Prithee, bring me
To the dead bodies of my queen and son: 235
One grave shall be for both: upon them shall
The causes of their death appear, unto

Leontes says that he will daily worship in the chapel where his wife and son are buried.

240 recreation: re-creation; a pun on the word which also suggests 'exercise' in the next line
nature: my body
241 exercise: spiritual devotions

Antigonus has arrived by boat on the coast of Bohemia where he plans to leave the baby in a desert place. The Mariner urges haste since a storm is expected. Antigonus has seen a vision of Hermione.

1 perfect: certain
2 deserts: wilderness, deserted place
4 present: immediate
In my conscience: to my mind
5 with that we have in hand: with what we are doing
8 bark: small sailing ship
11 loud: stormy

> • *Do lines 16–18 provide further evidence that Hermione is dead? In what ways are they less than convincing?*

Our shame perpetual. Once a day I'll visit
The chapel where they lie, and tears shed there
Shall be my recreation. So long as nature   240
Will bear up with this exercise, so long
I daily vow to use it. Come, and lead me
To these sorrows.   [*Exeunt*

Scene 3

Enter ANTIGONUS *with the* BABE, *and a* MARINER

ANTIGONUS	Thou art perfect, then, our ship hath touched upon The deserts of Bohemia?
MARINER	Ay, my lord, and fear We have landed in ill time: the skies look grimly, And threaten present blusters. In my conscience, The heavens with that we have in hand are angry, 5 And frown upon 's.
ANTIGONUS	Their sacred wills be done! Go, get aboard; Look to thy bark: I'll not be long before I call upon thee.
MARINER	Make your best haste, and go not 10 Too far i' th' land: 'tis like to be loud weather; Besides, this place is famous for the creatures Of prey that keep upon 't.
ANTIGONUS	Go thou away: I'll follow instantly.
MARINER	I am glad at heart To be so rid o' th' business. [*Exit*
ANTIGONUS	Come, poor babe: 15 I have heard, but not believed, the spirits o' th' dead May walk again: if such thing be, thy mother Appeared to me last night; for ne'er was dream So like a waking. To me comes a creature,

Antigonus recounts his vision in which Hermione has instructed him to bring the baby to Bohemia. The child is to be called Perdita. Antigonus will not see his wife, Paulina, again. He believes that the vision is a sign that Hermione is dead and that the instructions come from Apollo. He lays Perdita, with details of her story, on the ground. The storm breaks.

20 some another: sometimes on the other

21 vessel: person, but the word is played upon to suggest both Hermione's tears, like an overflowing bowl (see line 26 below), and her robes like the sails of the ship where he saw her and upon which he now looks

23 sanctity: saintliness

28 better disposition: well-argued case; good inclinations – the spirit puns on two usages of the phrase

30 according to thine oath: the oath he swore to Leontes, his king. The spirit does not ask him to break this sacred oath.

33 Perdita: from the Latin, meaning 'that which is lost'

34 For this ungentle: because of this dishonourable

39 toys: trifling things

41 squared: directed

47 character: writing; documents which identify her (see Act 5 scene 2 lines 35–36)
   these: pieces of gold in a box, which Antigonus lays beside the baby and his letters (see lines 115–121 below)

48–49 both breed...thine: be sufficient both to pay for your upbringing, pretty child, and provide always for you

51 To loss: to being lost
   Weep I cannot: a reference to his dream – see above, line 32

- *In what ways might the storm have symbolic significance?*

Sometimes her head on one side, some another;　20
I never saw a vessel of like sorrow,
So filled, and so becoming: in pure white robes,
Like very sanctity, she did approach
My cabin where I lay: thrice bowed before me,
And, gasping to begin some speech, her eyes　25
Became two spouts. The fury spent, anon
Did this break from her: 'Good Antigonus,
Since fate, against thy better disposition,
Hath made thy person for the thrower-out
Of my poor babe, according to thine oath,　30
Places remote enough are in Bohemia,
There weep, and leave it crying: and, for the babe
Is counted lost for ever, Perdita,
I prithee, call 't. For this ungentle business,
Put on thee by my lord, thou ne'er shalt see　35
Thy wife Paulina more.' And so, with shrieks,
She melted into air. Affrighted much,
I did in time collect myself, and thought
This was so, and no slumber. Dreams are toys:
Yet for this once, yea, superstitiously,　40
I will be squared by this. I do believe
Hermione hath suffered death; and that
Apollo would, this being indeed the issue
Of King Polixenes, it should here be laid,
Either for life or death, upon the earth　45
Of its right father. Blossom, speed thee well!
There lie, and there thy character: there these,
Which may, if fortune please, both breed thee,
　　pretty,
And still rest thine. The storm begins: poor
　　wretch,
That for thy mother's fault art thus exposed　50
To loss and what may follow! Weep I cannot,
But my heart bleeds; and most accursed am I
To be by oath enjoined to this. Farewell!

Amidst the storm a bear is being hunted. Antigonus is set upon by the bear and exits. The Old Shepherd enters, observes the wild hunt but then sees the baby. He speculates on its origins and decides to rescue it. His son enters.

57 the chase: the hunt

58 Stage direction Real bears were used for entertainment in England at this time. They were made to dance and perform tricks as well as being used in bear-baiting pits where bets were placed on their combat with dogs. It has been suggested that a bear from the pit close to the Globe Theatre on Bankside was used in the performance (see below, line 129 and note).

64 boiled-brains: hot-heads or fools: the words are not synonymous but the Shepherd's comments rather suggest both conditions.

67 I have them: I shall find them

68–69 and 't Be thy will: if it is thy (God's) will

70 barne: bairn; child

71 child: girl; like 'barne' in the previous line this is a dialect usage and establishes the Shepherd's rural credentials

72 scape: escapade or sexual sin

74–75 stair-work...behind-door-work: 'work' is a euphemism for sexual intercourse; the stairs, trunk and door suggest either where the deed took place or the lover's means of access to the waiting-gentlewoman, though they perhaps owe most to the Shepherd's imaginative view of life amongst the aristocracy

76 got: begot, conceived

78 hallooed: shouted

80 What, art so near?: the Clown's entry is often used as an opportunity for visual comedy; father and son may, for example, slowly back into each other while shouting loudly towards opposite wings. The laughter is sustained by the Shepherd's next comment and the Clown's inability to tell a plain tale.

• *'Exit, pursued by a bear' is a famous Shakespearean stage direction, but how would you carry it out? Should the audience be alarmed or encouraged to laugh at this moment in the play?*

The day frowns more and more: thou 'rt like to
  have
A lullaby too rough: I never saw   55
The heavens so dim by day. A savage clamour!
Well may I get aboard! This is the chase:
I am gone for ever!   [*Exit, pursued by a bear*

Enter the OLD SHEPHERD

SHEPHERD   I would there were no age between ten and three-
            and-twenty, or that youth would sleep out the   60
            rest; for there is nothing in the between but getting
            wenches with child, wronging the ancientry,
            stealing, fighting – Hark you now! Would any but
            these boiled-brains of nineteen and two-and twenty
            hunt this weather? They have scared away two   65
            of my best sheep, which I fear the wolf will sooner
            find than the master: if anywhere I have them, 'tis
            by the sea-side, browzing of ivy. Good luck, and 't
            Be thy will. [*Seeing the babe*] What have we here?
            Mercy on 's a barne! A very pretty barne! A   70
            boy or a child, I wonder? A pretty one; a very pretty
            one. Sure, some scape: though I am not bookish,
            yet I can read waiting-gentlewoman in the scape.
            This has been some stair-work, some trunk-work,
            some behind-door-work: they were warmer   75
            that got this than the poor thing is here. I'll take it
            up for pity: yet I'll tarry till my son come; he
            hallooed but even now. Whoa-ho-hoa!

            Enter CLOWN

CLOWN   Hilloa, loa!

SHEPHERD   What, art so near? If thou'lt see a thing to talk   80
            on when thou art dead and rotten, come hither.
            What ail'st thou man?

CLOWN   I have seen two such sights, by sea and by land! But
            I am not to say it is a sea, for it is now the sky:

The Clown recounts the destruction of Antigonus by the
bear and of his ship by the storm. Shepherd and Clown
regret they could not save anyone. The Shepherd shows the
baby to his son and together they open the box which
Antigonus left with the child.

85 firmament: sky; heavens

86 bodkin: large needle

93 yest: yeast; the Clown is thinking of ale foaming from a
barrel

94 hogs-head: barrel

95 land-service: (as opposed to the naval service) – the events
at sea which he has been describing. 'Service' then suggests
the meal which is being served up to the bear.

98–99 flap-dragoned: gulped down; a flap-dragon was a
brandy-soaked raisin which was eaten having been first set
alight

104 winked: blinked

109–111 I would...footing: the Clown indignantly suggests
that an attempt to save either Antigonus or the ship would
have been equally ill-founded

115–116 a bearing-cloth for a squire's child: in commenting
upon Hermione's mantle (see Act 5 scene 2 line 33) the
Shepherd again betrays his innocence of the courtly life

118 changeling: a fairy child left in exchange for a stolen human
baby

- *'Thou met'st with things dying, I with things new-
  born' (lines 113–114): this antithesis – rhetorical
  contrast – is a turning point in the play. The emotions,
  values and language of the first half of the play are
  about to be replaced by a new and largely contrary
  view of the world.*

	betwixt the firmament and it you cannot thrust 85 a bodkin's point.
SHEPHERD	Why, boy, how is it?
CLOWN	I would you did see how if chafes, how it rages, how it takes up the shore! But that's not to the point. O, the most piteous cry of the poor souls! 90 Sometimes to see 'em, and not to see 'em: now the ship boring the moon with her main-mast, and anon swallowed with yest and froth, as you 'd thrust a cork into a hogs-head. And then for the land-service, to see how the bear tore out his 95 shoulder-bone, how he cried to me for help and said his name was Antigonus, a nobleman. But to make an end of the ship, to see how the sea flap- dragoned it: but first, how the poor souls roared, and the sea mocked them: and how the poor 100 gentleman roared, and the bear mocked him, both roaring louder than the sea or weather.
SHEPHERD	Name of mercy, when was this, boy?
CLOWN	Now, now: I have not winked since I saw these sights: the men are not yet cold under water, nor 105 the bear half dined on the gentleman: he's at it now.
SHEPHERD	Would I had been by, to have helped the old man!
CLOWN	I would you had been by the ship side, to have helped her: there your charity would have lacked 110 footing.
SHEPHERD	Heavy matters! heavy matters! But look thee here, boy. Now bless thyself: thou met'st with things dying, I with things new-born. Here's a sight for thee; look thee, a bearing-cloth for a 115 squire's child! Look thee here; take up, take up, boy; open 't. So, let's see: it was told me I should be rich by the fairies. This is some changeling: open 't. What's within, boy?
CLOWN	You're a made old man: if the sins of your youth 120

Shepherd and Clown find the gold which, like Perdita, they assume to be a gift from the fairies. To retain it they believe they must keep it a secret. The Clown departs to bury Antigonus.

121 **you're well to live**: you will live well, prosperously
122 **fairy gold**: and thus likely to vanish or bring bad luck if spoken about to others
124 **still**: always
129 **curst**: bad-tempered. The Clown's apparent knowledge of the behaviour of bears has led some commentators to suggest that this is evidence that a real bear was used in the performance (see above, line 58 and note, and also Act 4 scene 4 line 815).

- *In what ways are the Shepherd's final words ironic?*

are forgiven you, you're well to live. Gold! All gold!

SHEPHERD This is fairy gold, boy, and 'twill prove so; up
with 't, keep it close: home, home, the next way.
We are lucky, boy; and to be so still requires
nothing but secrecy. Let my sheep go: come,   125
good boy, the next way home.

CLOWN Go you the next way with your findings. I'll go see
if the bear be gone from the gentleman, and how
much he hath eaten; they are never curst but when
they are hungry: if there be any of him left, I'll   130
bury it.

SHEPHERD That's a good deed. If thou mayest discern by that
which is left of him what he is, fetch me to th' sight
of him.

CLOWN Marry, will I; and you shall help to put him i' th' 135
ground.

SHEPHERD 'Tis a lucky day, boy, and we'll do good deeds
on 't.   [*Exeunt*

Keeping track

Scene 1

1 What was the reaction of Cleomenes and Dion to the Oracle?
2 How do they feel towards:
   • Hermione
   • Leontes?

Scene 2

1 What are the reasons that Leontes gives for holding an open trial?
2 How does Hermione reply to the charges made against her?
3 Write down the phrases in Hermione's speech (lines 91–116) when she refers to the following.
   • Life does not mean much to her.
   • She has lost the favour of Leontes.
   • She has been forbidden to see Mamillius.
   • Her baby daughter has been torn from her.
   • She has been given no rest after the birth of her child.
4 What is written in the 'sealed-up Oracle' (line 127)?
5 • What is Leontes' immediate reaction to the Oracle?
   • How does he then react when he learns of Mamillius' death?
6 How does Paulina break the news of Hermione's 'death'?
7 Why does Paulina request punishment (lines 220–232)?
8 In Leontes' last speech in the scene, what does he resolve to do?

Scene 3

1 Why, according to the mariner, does the storm break upon Antigonus and the ship?
2 Antigonus describes his dream (lines 19–36). Recount it in your own words.
3 What does Antigonus leave with the baby (lines 47 and 114–121)?
4 What is the Shepherd complaining about in his first speech?
5 What, according to the Shepherd, are the reasons for the baby being there? (Look at lines 72–76 and 118.)
6 How does Shakespeare ensure that no-one will come forward as a witness to the exposure of Perdita to the elements?
7 How is some dignity restored to Antigonus at the end of the scene?

Characters

Leontes

Leontes' transformation and repentance in Act 3 is as sudden as his initial descent into jealousy and cruelty.
1 What stages does he go through?
2 Do you find these changes convincing?

Hermione

At her trial Hermione does not attempt to prove her innocence.
1 How does she counter Leontes' accusations?
2 What are the strengths and weaknesses of this defence?
3 Why does she behave in this way?

Paulina

1 What does Paulina do in scene 2?
2 She has to convince the audience that Hermione is dead. Do you believe her? Why? (You may find it helpful to have tried DRAMA activity 3 below.)

The Old Shepherd and the Clown

1 What differences in character do you detect between these two?
2 How are the differences demonstrated?
3 What is your reaction to the clown's manner of speech – especially in his description of the death of Antigonus and the wreck of the ship? What are the characteristics of his style and imagery?
4 What is the effect of the appearance of these two characters on the mood of the play?

Themes

1 Make a list of the examples of *deceit* and *deception* in this act, indicating whether you think the intention of each example is for good or bad.
2 What elements of this act do you find fantastic or improbable? What elements are realistic or believable?

Drama

1 **Scene 2 lines 1–123**
The class should divide into two groups. One group becomes the prosecution team, and the other is the team defending Hermione.

- Assemble arguments, using the evidence of Hermione's behaviour in the previous scenes. Look, too, at the arguments used during this scene and try to suggest others.
- Either one of the class or the teacher could in turn adopt the roles of the king and queen who receive and challenge the advice of their lawyers.

2 Scene 2 lines 124–154

In these lines there is a series of shocks and declarations. We shall explore how the various characters react by staging the scene. Work as a whole class.

- Cast the parts.
- Read the lines aloud.
- Set out the courtroom and establish where the entrances are.
- Work out the sequence of arrivals.
- Consider how each character or group responds to each new statement.
- Try the whole scene, developing the pattern of movements and intensifying the dramatic impact.

3 Scene 2 lines 175–202

Paulina's speech builds up to the climactic revelation that the queen is dead. Use FORUM THEATRE techniques (see page 263) to examine the moment of climax:

'the queen, the queen,
The sweet'st dear'st creature's dead' (lines 200–201).

- Look at the structure of the lines to see if Shakespeare is giving directions as to where the emphases should be.
- Is Paulina out of breath by this point?
- Is Leontes beaten to the ground by her list of his crimes?
- Is Paulina telling the truth?
- What are the Lords doing ?

4 Scene 3

How should the baby and the bear be portrayed? There have been productions in which the baby has been played by a real baby (or series of babies) – some of whom cried and others who stayed asleep! A real bear might prove even more of a problem: various productions have used shadows or large actors in bear costumes. How does a production manage to move from the atmosphere of tragedy and sadness to the humour of the clowns? Is the bear part of the tragedy or part of the fun – or is it partly both?

- Working in a group of four, imagine you are a production team. Argue for your particular interpretation of these issues and come to an agreed solution which you can 'sell' to the rest of the class.

Close study

Scene 3 lines 15–58

1   What phrases convince us of the powerful effect of the vision upon Antigonus?

2   What descriptive words and imagery are used to describe:
    • Hermione
    • Perdita?
    In what ways are these words significant?

3   Why does Antigonus leave the baby exposed? How far do you sympathize with his reasoning?

4   Remind yourself of the way that you viewed the character of Antigonus in Act 2 scenes 1 and 2. Are there any differences between the way that he spoke and acted during those scenes and the way that we see him now?

5   Antigonus' death is an unusual one. Why does he have to die? What is the dramatic impact of his death?

6   Despite the storm and the hunt, Antigonus' speech is controlled. What features of the language, sentence construction and rhythm achieve this effect?

Key scene

Act 3 scene 2

Dramatically this scene is one of the most important in the play because it is, in effect, the end of a chain of events. After this scene the story is concerned with the consequences of those events.

Keying it in

1   Make a list of the actions of Leontes and others which have led up to this moment.

2   Look again at Act 1 scene 2 lines 334–341, Act 2 scene 1 lines 180–198, Act 2 scene 3 lines 1–26 and 197–206. What do these extracts tell you about Leontes' motives for bringing Hermione to trial and the outcome which he expects? Can she receive a fair trial?

The scene itself

1   Lines 1–8

    • Summarize the main points of this speech.
    • What is significant about Leontes' choice of words?

2 Lines 22–54

Hermione replies to the charges against her.

- Summarize her argument (or refer to the answer you wrote to 'Keeping track' scene 2 question 2).
- The dignified effect of her words is partly due to the rhythmical balance of her phrases, for example in lines 30–32. Find and note other examples of this balance.
- Rhythm is also emphasized by alliteration. Find examples of alliteration used in this way.

3 Lines 54–76

- What does Hermione say about Polixenes and Camillo?
- How does she emphasize her past loyalty to her husband?

4 Lines 77–116

Hermione emphasizes what she has lost and why life does not mean much to her now.

- How does she do this?
- What does she prize above everything else?
- What has Hermione said which is calculated to gain the audience's sympathy?

5 Lines 116–153

The text of the Oracle reveals the truth and offers no way forward unless '*that which is lost be not found*' (lines 135–136). Leontes pronounces that the Oracle is wrong.

- What actions and words increase the drama of this moment?
- What is the link between what Leontes says in lines 146 and 147 and Act 3 scene 3?

6 Lines 153–172

Leontes' repentance is immediate. How does the style of his speech now contrast with what we have come to expect from him?

7 Lines 172–214

Paulina takes a long time to get to the point.

- Summarize the stages in her speech.
- What different emotions does she seem to go through?
- What is the evidence that the effect of her speech is carefully calculated?

8 Lines 214–232

Consider the tone of Paulina's speech.

- How has it changed from the previous speech?
- How would you describe Paulina's intentions here?

- Is she concerned to guide Leontes' reaction in a particular way?

Lines 232–243
- What does Leontes decide to do?
- Do you think that his reaction is as intemperate and irrational as his earlier jealousy, or is it justifiable?

verview

⦁ With whom do you sympathize at the end of this scene? Why?

'riting

During Act 3 there are abrupt changes between three different settings and even more emotional states. Summarize these changes and their impact on the audience.

Imagine that Shakespeare ended the play after Act 3 scene 2 and that you have been commissioned to provide an ending. *Either* write an outline which satisfactorily concludes the story *or* justify the suggestion that Act 3 scene 2 is itself a satisfactory conclusion.

Time, a Chorus, tells how sixteen years have passed in the li[ve]
of the characters. Though he asks the audience to have
patience with this narrative leap, he makes no apology since,
says, we are all subject to Time. He introduces Polixenes' so[n]
Florizel. He tells us that Leontes grieves in seclusion while
Perdita has grown up.

> **Stage direction** *the* CHORUS: Shakespeare uses the Chorus
> here, as in some other plays, to comment on the action and [to]
> fill in narrative which it would be impossible or undesirable [to]
> dramatize. However, the Chorus is also characterized as Tim[e]
> a crucial agent in the development of the story, and so appea[rs]
> in conventional guise with wings and hour-glass.
> 1 **try all**: test everyone
> 2 **unfolds**: reveals; resolves. The sense of this opening couplet [is]
>   Time pleases some people and tests everyone – since the goo[d]
>   and the bad things of life offer both joy and terror – and it t[a]
>   time to both make and resolve errors.
> 4 **Impute it not**: do not say that it is
> 6–7 **and leave...gap**: and leave the developments of that long
>   period unexamined
> 8, 9 **law, custom**: Time refers to the Aristotelian dramatic the[ory]
>   of the unities of time, place and action. Since Time has itself
>   become a character in the play he now gives himself licence [to]
>   disobey inconvenient rules.
> 9 **plant and o'erwhelm**: create and destroy
> 10–11 **ere ancient'st...received**: see lines 8 and 9 above. The
>   Ancient Greek writings had been 'received' and adapted by
>   sixteenth-century playwrights and commentators.
> 13–15 **make stale...to it**: in the future I shall make these
>   glittering present days seem as old-fashioned as my play mus[t]
>   now seem by comparison with present reality.
> 16 **my glass**: see note on stage direction, above.
> 17 **As**: as if
> 18 **fond**: foolish
> 25 **Equal with wond'ring**: equal to the wonder she inspired i[n]
>   those (simple country people) who saw her grow up
> 26 **I list not**: I choose not to
> 28 **what to her adheres**: what belongs to her story

Act four

cene **1**

Enter TIME, *the* CHORUS

IME   I that please some, try all: both joy and terror
Of good and bad, that makes and unfolds error,
Now take upon me, in the name of Time,
To use my wings. Impute it not a crime
To me, or my swift passage, that I slide   5
O'er sixteen years, and leave the growth untried
Of that wide gap, since it is in my power
To o'erthrow law, and in one self-born hour
To plant and o'erwhelm custom. Let me pass
The same I am, ere ancient'st order was,   10
Or what is now received. I witness to
The times that brought them in; so shall I do
To th' freshest things now reigning, and make stale
The glistering of this present, as my tale
Now seems to it. Your patience this allowing,   15
I turn my glass, and give my scene such growing
As you had slept between. Leontes leaving,
Th' effects of his fond jealousies so grieving
That he shuts up himself, imagine me,
Gentle spectators, that I now may be   20
In fair Bohemia, and remember well
I mentioned a son o' th' king's, which Florizel
I now name to you; and with speed so pace
To speak of Perdita, now grown in grace
Equal with wond'ring. What of her ensues   25
I list not prophesy; but let Time's news
Be known when 'tis brought forth. A shepherd's
    daughter,
And what to her adheres, which follows after,

The Chorus promises that the story he is about to unfold
will be worth spending time on.

29 th'argument: the subject

29–32 Of this allow...may: if you have ever spent time worse
before you saw this play, allow the rest of it to be performed
now; if you have never spent time worse, allow me to say that
I hope you never will in the future

Bohemia. Polixenes enters with Camillo who has asked
permission to visit Sicilia. He wishes to see Leontes and to
die in his own country. Polixenes persuades him to stay,
telling him that he is indispensable. The king does not wish
to be reminded of Sicilia: Florizel, however, is very much on
his mind.

2 importunate: persistent in making a request
  'tis a sickness: it is painful to me

3 a death: but it would kill me

4 fifteen: presumably an error since elsewhere Time, Paulina
  and Camillo make the gap sixteen years

5 been aired abroad: lived and breathed in foreign countries

8–9 be some allay...so: be some comfort, or so I presume to
  think

13 want: lack

14 made me businesses: conducted affairs of state

18 considered: rewarded

20 the heaping friendships: the accumulation of more friendly
  service

24 brother: that is, fellow king

> • *What indications are there that Polixenes is an
>   emotional man?*

Is th' argument of Time. Of this allow,
If ever you have spent time worse ere now;   30
If never, yet that Time himself doth say,
He wishes earnestly you never may.   [*Exit*

Scene 2

Enter POLIXENES *and* CAMILLO

POLIXENES   I pray thee, good Camillo, be no more
importunate: 'tis a sickness denying thee anything;
a death to grant this.

CAMILLO   It is fifteen years since I saw my country: though I
have, for the most part, been aired abroad, I   5
desire to lay my bones there. Besides, the penitent
king, my master, hath sent for me; to whose feeling
sorrows I might be some allay (or I o'erween to
think so), which is another spur to my departure.

POLIXENES   As thou lov'st me, Camillo, wipe not out the   10
rest of thy services by leaving me now: the need I
have of thee, thine own goodness hath made; better
not to have had thee than thus to want thee. Thou,
having made me businesses, which none without
thee can sufficiently manage, must either stay to   15
execute them thyself, or take away with thee the
very services thou hast done: which if I have not
enough considered (as too much I cannot), to be
more thankful to thee shall be my study; and my
profit therein, the heaping friendships. Of that   20
fatal country, Sicilia, prithee speak no more; whose
very naming punishes me with the remembrance of
that penitent (as thou call'st him) and reconciled
king, my brother; whose loss of his most precious
queen and children are even now to be afresh   25
lamented. Say to me, when sawest thou the Prince
Florizel, my son? Kings are no less unhappy, their

Camillo notes that Florizel is often missing from Court. Polixenes' spies have discovered that the Prince is spending time at the house of the Shepherd where it appears that Perdita is the attraction. Polixenes tells Camillo to accompany him in disguise to the Shepherd's home.

29 approved: proved. Having been reminded of Sicilia, Polixenes appears to be making a comparison between his own son's behaviour and the promised graciousness of the dead Mamillius.

32 (missingly) noted: noted his absence precisely because he has been missing

33–34 princely exercises: royal duties

36 so far that I have eyes: to the extent that I have spies

37 look upon his removedness: watch his movements while away from court

39 homely: unsophisticated

41–42 an unspeakable estate: indescribable wealth

44 of most rare note: extraordinarily noteworthy

47 intelligence: information, secretly obtained

48 angle: fishhook

49–50 not appearing what we are: in disguise

• *Why, do you think, is this scene in prose?*

issue not being gracious, than they are in losing
them when they have approved their virtues.

CAMILLO   Sir, it is three days since I saw the Prince. What   30
his happier affairs may be, are to me unknown: but
I have (missingly) noted, he is of late much retired
from court, and is less frequent to his princely
exercises than formerly he hath appeared.

POLIXENES I have considered so much, Camillo, and with   35
some care; so far that I have eyes under my service
which look upon his removedness; from whom I
have this intelligence, that he is seldom from the
house of a most homely shepherd; a man, they say,
that from very nothing, and beyond the   40
imagination of his neighbours, is grown into an
unspeakable estate.

CAMILLO   I have heard, sir, of such a man, who hath a
daughter of most rare note: the report of her is
extended more than can be thought to begin   45
from such a cottage.

POLIXENES That's likewise part of my intelligence: but, I fear,
the angle that plucks our son thither. Thou shalt
accompany us to the place, where we will (not
appearing what we are) have some question with   50
the shepherd; from whose simplicity I think it not
uneasy to get the cause of my son's resort thither.
Prithee, be my present partner in this business, and
lay aside the thoughts of Sicilia.

CAMILLO   I willingly obey your command.   55

POLIXENES My best Camillo! We must disguise ourselves.

                                              [*Exeunt*

Autolycus enters singing joyfully of spring, of women and of thieving. He is a former servant of Florizel but now lives by theft and trickery.

> **Stage direction** *AUTOLYCUS*: in Greek mythology Autolycus is one of the sons of Hermes (Mercury). He is a thief with magical powers. His name literally means 'the wolf itself'.
>
> **1 peer**: appear, or perhaps peep
>
> **2 doxy**: beggar's mistress
>
> **3 sweet**: the best part
>
> **4 pale**: pale cheeks, with a play on 'pale' meaning a protected enclosure where the reign of Winter is replaced by Spring
>
> **7 set my pugging tooth on edge**: whet my appetite for theft. To pug is to pull, as in pulling the sheets from the hedges in order to steal them; tooth here means taste, sharpened like a knife which has been given an edge.
>
> **11 aunts**: women, whores
>
> **14 three-pile**: expensive velvet
>
> **18 I then do most go right**: Autolycus contrasts the freedom of the thief and vagabond with the discipline of the court servant: to be conventionally 'right' is for him wrong
>
> **19–22 If tinkers...avouch it**: if tinkers (itinerant menders of pots and pans) are allowed to practise their trade, carrying their tools in a pigskin bag, then I can give an equally good account of myself and when I am put in the stocks I shall swear that I tell the truth. There were harsh laws against beggars and vagabonds so Autolycus also carries a budget as sign that he is a tradesman.
>
> **23–24 My traffic is...linen**: my speciality is stolen sheets; when the kite builds its nest, look after your small linen articles which it may steal to line its nest (but when I'm around, lining my nest, look out for the sheets!)
>
> **25 littered under Mercury**: born under the astrological sign of the planet Mercury; see note on Autolycus, above
>
> **26 unconsidered**: neglected; unwatched
>
> **27 die and drab**: gambling and prostitutes (were my downfall)
> **this caparison**: these clothes
>
> **27–28 my revenue...cheat**: I make money from simple, petty theft and by cheating foolish people
>
> **28 knock**: beatings

Scene 3

Enter AUTOLYCUS, *singing*

When daffodils begin to peer,
    With heigh! the doxy over the dale,
Why then comes in the sweet o' the year,
    For the red blood reigns in the winter's pale.

The white sheet bleaching on the hedge,   5
    With hey! the sweet birds, O how they sing!
Doth set my pugging tooth on edge;
    For a quart of ale is a dish for a king.

The lark, that tirra-lirra chants,
    With heigh! with heigh! the thrush and the
        jay,   10
Are summer songs for me and my aunts,
    While we lie tumbling in the hay.

I have served Prince Florizel, and in my time wore
three-pile, but now I am out of service.

But shall I go mourn for that, my dear?   15
    The pale moon shines by night:
And when I wander here and there,
    I then do most go right.

If tinkers may have leave to live,
    And bear the sow-skin budget,   20
Then my account I well may give,
    And in the stocks avouch it.

My traffic is sheets; when the kite builds, look to
lesser linen. My father named me Autolycus; who
being, as I am, littered under Mercury, was   25
likewise a snapper-up of unconsidered trifles. With
die and drab I purchased this caparison, and my
revenue is the silly cheat. Gallows and knock are
too powerful on the highway: beating and hanging

The Clown enters, having been sent by Perdita to shop for
groceries in preparation for the sheep-shearing feast. She has
been made mistress of what will clearly be a lavish occasion.
The Clown is not short of money but finds the arithmetic
difficult. Autolycus recognizes him as easy pickings and rolls
around on the ground pretending to have been mugged.

30–31 for the life...of it: as for the future (both in this world
and the next), I don't think about it

32–33 every 'leven wether...shilling: every eleven sheep yields
28 lb (a tod) of wool; every tod will sell for 21 shillings
(£1.05). A wether is a castrated male sheep.

34 what comes the wool to?: much of England's wealth was
based upon wool and the export of cloth. The audience
would have enjoyed the topical reference and probably
shouted out the answer.

35 If the springe...mine: if the snare is strong enough the
foolish young man is mine. Woodcock were proverbially
stupid birds.

41 lays it on: does it, with a suggestion of over-doing it

42 nosegays: bunches of sweet-smelling flowers (to suppress bad
smells and the diseases they were thought to spread)
three-man song-men: singers of three-part songs for male
voices

44 means and basses: middle and lower voices – that is, tenors
and basses but not altos

44–45 but one puritan...hornpipes: except for one of them
who is a puritan who would even sing the words of a psalm to
a hornpipe (a lively dance tune)

46 saffron: orange-yellow flower used for food colouring
warden pies: pies made from warden pears
mace: spice made from the dried outer covering of nutmeg

47 out of my note: not on my list

48 race: root

49–50 o' th' sun: dried in the open air

52 I' th' name of me!: the Clown avoids using the name of god
in an oath (forbidden in the theatre at this time) but invents
an appropriately foolish alternative

58 stripes: lashes of a whip

60–61 come to a great matter: amount to a considerable thing

	are terrors to me: for the life to come, I sleep 30
	out the thought of it. A prize! a prize!

Enter CLOWN

CLOWN	Let me see: every 'leven wether tods; every tod
	yields pound and odd shilling. Fifteen hundred
	shorn, what comes the wool to?
AUTOLYCUS	[*Aside*] If the springe hold, the cock's mine. 35
CLOWN	I cannot do 't without counters. Let me see;
	what am I to buy for our sheep-shearing feast?
	Three pound of sugar, five pound of currants, rice –
	what will this sister of mine do with rice? But my
	father hath made her mistress of the feast, and 40
	she lays it on. She hath made me four-and-twenty
	nosegays for the shearers, three-man song-men all,
	and very good ones; but they are most of them
	means and basses but one puritan amongst them,
	and he sings psalms to hornpipes. I must have 45
	saffron to colour the warden pies; mace; dates,
	none – that's out of my note; nutmegs, seven; a
	race or two of ginger, but that I may beg; four
	pound of prunes, and as many of raisins o' th'
	sun. 50
AUTOLYCUS	O that ever I was born! [*Grovelling on the ground*
CLOWN	I' th' name of me!
AUTOLYCUS	O, help me, help me! pluck but off these rages; and
	then, death, death!
CLOWN	Alack, poor soul! thou hast need of more rags to 55
	lay on thee, rather than have these off.
AUTOLYCUS	O sir, the loathsomeness of them offends me more
	than the stripes I have received, which are mighty
	ones and millions.
CLOWN	Alas, poor man! a million of beating may come 60
	to a great matter.
AUTOLYCUS	I am robbed, sir, and beaten; my money and

The Clown helps Autolycus who picks his pocket. Autolycus describes the man who, he claims, has robbed him. He appears to be describing himself.

65 a horseman, or a footman: a mounted highwayman or a footpad

69 very hot service: many fierce fights

77 a charitable office: a generous service

78–79 Dost lack...beseech you, sir: the Clown's generous response is ironic; presumably he reaches for his purse and Autolycus is quick to stop him

86 troll-my-dames: Autolycus plays on two senses: troumadame was a game, similar to bagatelle, sometimes used for gambling; trulls were prostitutes. He is reminding himself that it was die and drab that undid him (see above, line 27).

88 virtues: a further example of his making wrongs into rights (see above, line 18)

92 but abide: than stay there briefly

94 ape-bearer: used a monkey for fairground entertainment
process-server: one who delivers writs, often a bailiff

95–96 compassed a motion...Son: acquired a puppet-show of the biblical parable of the Prodigal Son; he is also suggesting that Autolycus partially reformed himself

> • *Autolycus is a wolf in sheep's clothing. What deceptions does he perpetrate here?*

	apparel ta'en from me, and these detestable things	
	put upon me.	
CLOWN	What, by a horseman, or a footman?	65
AUTOLYCUS	A footman, sweet sir, a footman.	
CLOWN	Indeed, he should be a footman by the garments he	
	has left with thee: if this be a horseman's coat, it	
	hath seen very hot service. Lend me thy hand, I'll	
	help thee: come, lend me thy hand.	70
AUTOLYCUS	O, good sir, tenderly, O!	
CLOWN	Alas, poor soul!	
AUTOLYCUS	O, good sir, softly, good sir! I fear, sir, my shoulder-	
	blade is out.	
CLOWN	How now? Canst stand?	75
AUTOLYCUS	Softly, dear sir [*Picks his pocket*]; good sir,	
	softly. You ha' done me a charitable office.	
CLOWN	Dost lack any money? I have a little money for thee.	
AUTOLYCUS	No, good sweet sir; no, I beseech you, sir: I have a	
	kinsman not past three-quarters of a mile hence,	80
	unto whom I was going: I shall there have	
	money, or anything I want: offer me no money, I	
	pray you; that kills my heart.	
CLOWN	What manner of fellow was he that robbed you?	
AUTOLYCUS	A fellow, sir, that I have known to go about with	85
	troll-my-dames: I knew him once a servant of	
	the prince: I cannot tell, good sir, for which of his	
	virtues it was, but he was certainly whipped out of	
	the court.	
CLOWN	His vices, you would say; there's no virtue	90
	whipped out of the court: they cherish it to make it	
	stay there; and yet it will no more but abide.	
AUTOLYCUS	Vices I would say, sir. I know this man well; he hath	
	been since an ape-bearer, then a process-server (a	
	bailiff), then he compassed a motion of the	95
	Prodigal Son, and married a tinker's wife within	

The Clown comments upon Autolycus' cowardice. The rogue makes a remarkable recovery from his injuries and the fool exits to buy his groceries without a penny in his pocket. Autolycus resolves to attend the sheep-shearing feast since any crowd offers him an opportunity for gain. He exits singing.

97 **living**: estate
100 **prig**: thief
101 **wakes**: festivities
    bear-baitings: see note to Act 3 scene 3 line 58
107–108 **I am false of heart**: my heart fails me – but Autolycus ironically comments upon himself
112–113 **pace softly**: walk slowly
115 **good-faced**: handsome
121 **cheat**: trick
121–122 **prove sheep**: show themselves to be foolish and easy victims. Autolycus sees himself as a wolf (see note on Autolycus at the beginning of this scene).
122 **unrolled**: struck off the register of thieves
125 **hent**: take hold of

- *Autolycus introduces the first music into the play. How does this and other elements of his behaviour change the mood of the narrative?*

a mile where my land and living lies; and, having
flown over many knavish professions, he settled
only in rogue. Some call him Autolycus.

CLOWN
Out upon him! Prig, for my life, prig: he haunts 100
wakes, fairs, and bear-baitings.

AUTOLYCUS
Very true, sir; he, sir, he: that's the rogue that put
me into this apparel.

CLOWN
Not a more cowardly rogue in all Bohemia: if you
had but looked big and spit at him, he 'd have   105
run.

AUTOLYCUS
I must confess to you, sir, I am no fighter: I am
false of heart that way; and that he knew, I warrant
him.

CLOWN
How do you now?   110

AUTOLYCUS
Sweet sir, much better than I was: I can stand, and
walk: I will even take my leave of you, and pace
softly towards my kinsman's.

CLOWN
Shall I bring thee on the way?

AUTOLYCUS
No, good-faced sir; no, sweet sir.   115

CLOWN
Then fare-thee-well: I must go buy spices for our
sheep-shearing.

[*Exit*

AUTOLYCUS
Prosper you, sweet sir! Your purse is not hot
enough to purchase your spice. I'll be with you
at your sheep shearing too: if I make not this   120
cheat bring out another, and the shearers prove
sheep, let me be unrolled, and my name put in the
book of virtue!

[*Song*] Jog on, jog on, the foot-path way,
                And merrily hent the stile-a: 125
         A merry heart goes all the day,
                Your sad tires in a mile-a.

[*Exit*

The sheep-shearing feast. Florizel, disguised as a shepherd,
accompanies Perdita who is dressed as Flora, goddess of
flowers. She is embarrassed by the masquerade; he is
delighted by her. Perdita is fearful that Polixenes might
discover them.

1 **weeds**: garments
2 **Flora**: the Roman goddess of flowers
3 **Peering in April's front**: appearing at the beginning of April
5 **on 't**: of it
6 **extremes**: exaggerated compliments
8 **mark o' th' land**: centre of everyone's attention
9 **swain's wearing**: shepherd's garments. In the light of what
  happens to these clothes later in the scene and of Florizel's
  words at lines 25–31 (below), he may be dressed as the god
  Apollo disguised as a shepherd (see also line 762 below:
  fantastical).
10 **pranked up**: dressed up too showily
10–14 **But that our...glass**: if it were not that at our feasts
  every table shares in the foolish behaviour and the guests
  accept it as customary I should blush to see you dressed as
  you are now and faint if I saw myself in a mirror; 'mess' may
  mean both the table (see Act 1 scene 2 line 227) and the food
  eaten
16 **afford**: give
17 **difference**: that is, in social status
  your greatness: someone of your high rank
22 **Vilely bound up**: wretchedly dressed, but Perdita refers also
  to Florizel's infatuation with her. The metaphor is taken from
  book-binding.
23 **flaunts**: fine costume
24 **Apprehend**: look forward to

- ***What do Perdita's language and tone tell us about her
  character?***

Scene 4

Enter FLORIZEL *and* PERDITA

FLORIZEL These your unusual weeds, to each part of you
Do give a life: no shepherdess, but Flora
Peering in April's front. This your sheep-shearing
Is as a meeting of the petty gods,
And you the queen on 't.

PERDITA   Sir: my gracious lord,   5
To chide at your extremes, it not becomes me –
O pardon, that I name them! Your high self,
The gracious mark o' th' land, you have obscured
With a swain's wearing, and me, poor lowly maid,
Most goddess-like pranked up. But that our
    feasts   10
In every mess have folly, and the feeders
Digest it with a custom, I should blush
To see you so attired; swoon, I think,
To show myself a glass.

FLORIZEL   I bless the time
When my good falcon made her flight across   15
Thy father's ground.

PERDITA   Now Jove afford you cause!
To me the difference forges dread (your greatness
Hath not been used to fear). Even now I tremble
To think your father, by some accident
Should pass this way, as you did. O the Fates!   20
How would he look, to see his work, so noble,
Vilely bound up? What would he say? Or how
Should I, in these my borrowed flaunts, behold
The sternness of his presence?

FLORIZEL   Apprehend
Nothing but jollity. The gods themselves,   25
Humbling their deities to love, have taken

Florizel attempts to calm Perdita's fears with flattery and
expressions of his love. She is sure that his love will end
when he recognizes the reality of his situation. Florizel
assures her of his faithfulness and desires her to be happy.
More guests enter including, in disguise, his father and
Camillo.

27–30 Jupiter Became...swain: Jupiter became a bull in order
to seduce Europa, Neptune changed himself into a ram and
the woman Theophane into a ewe before he tupped her, and
Apollo roamed the woods in fruitless pursuit of the nymph,
Daphne

33 Nor in a way so chaste: nor were their intentions as chaste as
mine

35 faith: faithfulness; promise to marry

38–40 One of these...life: one of two courses will be necessary
and will have to be spoken of: either you must change your
mind or I will change the type of life I lead (because of your
determination to marry me). Perdita's words have a darker
implication, however: that her relationship with Florizel will
lead to her changing life for death.

41 forced: strained; far-fetched

42–43 Or I'll...father's: either I'll be your husband or I will
reject my father (and the kingdom)

46 gentle: dear friend – not an instruction but his mode of
address to her

47–48 with anything...while: with all the merrymaking of this
day

50 nuptial: marriage

52 Stand you auspicious: show us your favour

> • *Perdita and Florizel debate deception and disguise.*
> *What differing views do they hold? With whom do you*
> *sympathize?*

The shapes of beasts upon them: Jupiter
Became a bull, and bellowed; the green Neptune
A ram, and bleated; and the fire-robed god,
Golden Apollo, a poor humble swain,   30
As I seem now. Their transformations
Were never for a piece of beauty rarer,
Nor in a way so chaste, since my desires
Run not before mine honour, nor my lusts
Burn hotter than my faith.

PERDITA   O, but sir,   35
Your resolution cannot hold when 'tis
Opposed, as it must be, by th' power of the king:
One of these two must be necessities,
Which then will speak, that you must change this
    purpose,
Or I my life.

FLORIZEL   Thou dearest Perdita,   40
With these forced thoughts, I prithee, darken not
The mirth o' th' feast. Or I'll be thine, my fair,
Or not my father's. For I cannot be
Mine own, nor anything to any, if
I be not thine. To this I am most constant,   45
Though destiny say no. Be merry, gentle,
Strangle such thoughts as these with anything
That you behold the while. Your guests are coming:
Lift up your countenance, as it were the day
Of celebration of that nuptial which   50
We two have sworn shall come.

PERDITA   O lady Fortune,
Stand you auspicious!

Enter SHEPHERD, CLOWN, MOPSA, DORCAS, *and
others, with the disguised* POLIXENES *and* CAMILLO

FLORIZEL   See, your guests approach:
Address yourself to entertain them sprightly,
And let's be red with mirth.

The Shepherd chides Perdita for not welcoming their guests She greets the disguised Polixenes and Camillo with posies evergreen plants symbolic of their age.

56 pantler: pantry maid

57 dame: mistress

60 On his: at his

62 to each one sip: propose a toast to each of her guests

63 a feasted one: a guest

65–66 These unknown friends...known: welcome these unknown friends since that is the way to make them real friends and better acquainted with us

74 rosemary, and rue: herbs and evergreen shrubs which had symbolic significance: rosemary (because of its lingering scent) for friendship and remembrance, rue for grace and repentance

75 Seeming and savour: appearance and scent

82 gillyvors: gillyflowers or pinks, of the same family as carnations and sometimes associated with immorality

83 nature's bastards: because the streaks are produced by cross breeding; they are hybrids and not pure bred

85 slips: cuttings

> • *The audience knows who Perdita is; none of the characters on stage do. How is the dramatic irony emphasized by her own words and those of the Shepherd?*

SHEPHERD   Fie, daughter! when my old wife lived upon   55
This day she was both pantler, butler, cook,
Both dame and servant; welcomed all, served all;
Would sing her song and dance her turn; now here
At upper end o' th' table, now i' th' middle;
On his shoulder, and his; her face o' fire   60
With labour, and the thing she took to quench it
She would to each one sip. You are retired,
As if you were a feasted one, and not
The hostess of the meeting: pray you, bid
These unknown friends to 's welcome; for it is   65
A way to make us better friends, more known.
Come, quench your blushes, and present yourself
That which you are, Mistress o' th' Feast. Come on,
And bid us welcome to your sheep-shearing,
As your good flock shall prosper.

PERDITA   [*To* POLIXENES]   Sir, welcome: 70
It is my father's will I should take on me
The hostess-ship o' th' day. [*To* CAMILLO] You're welcome, sir.
Give me those flowers there, Dorcas. Reverend sirs,
For you, there's rosemary, and rue; these keep
Seeming and savour all the winter long: 75
Grace and remembrance be to you both,
And welcome to our shearing!

POLIXENES   Shepherdess –
A fair one are you – well you fit our ages
With flowers of winter.

PERDITA   Sir, the year growing ancient,
Not yet on summer's death nor on the birth   80
Of trembling winter, the fairest flowers o' th' season
Are our carnations and streaked gillyvors,
Which some call nature's bastards: of that kind
Our rustic garden's barren; and I care not
To get slips of them.

Perdita and Polixenes debate the relationship between
Nature and Art. He advocates the role of Art in perfecting
Nature; she maintains that this is a deception. Embarrassed
by her own boldness she gives Polixenes and Camillo
midsummer flowers to placate them.

87 piedness: variegated colouring

88–90 Say there be...that mean: even supposing that were
true, Nature is only improved by means which Nature
herself has made

93 gentler scion: noble descendant

94 bark: tree

101 were I painted: were I wearing make-up – which was
commonly associated with immorality at this time

103 you: probably Polixenes and Camillo; there is no need to
assume that Perdita offers flowers to other middle-aged men
at this point since the gifts are made to cover her
embarrassment at her previous gifts of winter flowers and
her forthright argument with Polixenes

104 Hot: plants were assumed to have temperatures and in
general those that flowered in spring were cold while all
those in the list which follows here bloom in high summer
and are hot

savory: a herb related to mint

106 with him rises, weeping: – since the marigold is
phototropic, opening and closing its flower with the sun's
rising and setting. In the morning it 'weeps' with dew.

> • *In lines 92–95 Polixenes describes very precisely how a
> gardener improves plants. What is ironic about these
> lines?*
> *(In* Richard II *Shakespeare compares a good king to a
> gardener who orders and prunes his plants, taming
> what is wild.)*

LIXENES   Wherefore, gentle maiden, 85
             Do you neglect them?

RDITA   For I have heard it said
             There is an art which, in their piedness, shares
             With great creating nature.

LIXENES   Say there be;
             Yet nature is made better by no mean
             But nature makes that mean: so, over that art, 90
             Which you say adds to nature, is an art
             That nature makes. You see, sweet maid, we marry
             A gentler scion to the wildest stock,
             And make conceive a bark of baser kind
             By bud of nobler race. This is an art 95
             Which does mend nature – change it rather – but
             The art itself is nature.

RDITA   So it is.

LIXENES   Then make your garden rich in gillyvors,
             And do not call them bastards.

RDITA   I'll not put
             The dibble in earth to set one slip of them; 100
             No more than, were I painted, I would wish
             This youth should say 'twere well, and only
                 therefore
             Desire to breed by me. Here's flowers for you:
             Hot lavender, mints, savory, marjoram,
             The marigold, that goes to bed wi' th' sun 105
             And with him rises, weeping: these are flowers
             Of middle summer, and I think they are given
             To men of middle age. Y'are very welcome.
                                    [*She gives them flowers*

MILLO   I should leave grazing, were I of your flock,
             And only live by gazing.

RDITA   Out, alas! 110
             You'd be so lean that blasts of January
             Would blow you through and through. Now, my
                 fair'st friend, [*To* FLORIZEL

Perdita regrets that, since it is late summer, she has no sprin
flowers to offer to Florizel and the Shepherdesses. She spea
warmly to Florizel of her love and once more finds herself
embarrassed by her own rashness. But Perdita can do no
wrong in the eyes of Florizel.

114 Become your time of day: suit your age

116 Proserpina: Proserpina, daughter of the goddess Ceres, w
gathering flowers when Dis (Pluto or Hades, god of the
underworld) abducted her in his chariot

120–122 dim, But sweeter...breath: demure, their heads
drooping more sweetly than the beautiful Juno's eyelids an
smelling sweeter than the breath of Cytherea (Venus)

122–125 pale primroses...maids: Shakespeare associates the
pale spring flower which dies before the summer sun
(Phoebus) reaches its zenith with anaemic 'green-sickness'
common in adolescent girls and from which some died. Th
waxy-green complexion of the girl was reminiscent of the
flower and it was supposed that girls who died of the illnes
lived on as primroses.

125 oxlips: a large, hence bold, hybrid form of the cowslip

126 crown imperial: the yellow fritillary, a lily-like flower then
recently introduced into England

127 flower-de-luce: fleur-de-lis, iris
these I lack: – because the sheep-shearing feast takes place
in midsummer

131 corpse: body, either living or dead

132 quick: alive; 'the quick and the dead' is a well-known
biblical antithesis

134 Whitsun pastorals: Whitsuntide (May) festivals might
include dramatic presentations of Robin Hood and Maid
Marion who were important figures in pastoral literature o
the period (see page 246–247)

136 Still betters what is done: always improves on the way
things are done by others

142 move still, still so: move now and always like that. Florize
plays on another sense of still: quiet, unmoving. This
paradox beautifully describes the timeless quality of the
finest music and dance.

I would I had some flowers o' th' spring, that
   might
Become your time of day; and yours, and yours,
                    [*To* MOPSA *and* DORCAS
That wear upon your virgin branches yet   115
Your maidenheads growing: O Proserpina,
For the flowers now that, frighted, thou let'st fall
From Dis's waggon! – daffodils,
That come before the swallow dares, and take
The winds of March with beauty; violets, dim,   120
But sweeter than the lids of Juno's eyes
Or Cytherea's breath; pale primroses,
That die unmarried, ere they can behold
Bright Phœbus in his strength (a malady
Most incident to maids); bold oxlips and   125
The crown imperial; lilies of all kinds,
The flower-de-luce being one. O, these I lack,
To make you garlands of, and my sweet friend,
To strew him o'er and o'er!

FLORIZEL   What, like a corpse?

PERDITA   No, like a bank, for love to lie and play on: 130
Not like a corpse; or if – not to be buried,
But quick, and in mine arms. Come, take your
   flowers:
Methinks I play as I have seen them do
In Whitsun pastorals: sure this robe of mine
Does change my disposition.

FLORIZEL   What you do,   135
Still betters what is done. When you speak, sweet,
I'd have you do it ever: when you sing,
I'd have you buy and sell so, so give alms,
Pray so, and, for the ord'ring your affairs,
To sing them too: when you do dance, I wish
   you   140
A wave o' th' sea, that you might ever do
Nothing but that, move still, still so,

Polixenes admires Perdita too and recognizes that her beauty and behaviour suggest nobility. With dancing about to begin, Dorcas, Mopsa and the Clown argue.

143 own no other function: have no other purpose in life

143–146 Each your doing...queens: everything you do, unique in every respect, is so supremely well done, moment by moment, that all your acts are like those of a queen

146 Doricles: Florizel's pastoral pseudonym which Shakespeare perhaps derived from Doris, one of the states of Ancient Greece (hence Doric and Dorian)

151–153 I think...to 't: Florizel reiterates his promise of lines 33–34 above

154 turtles: turtle-doves, which mate for life and are a conventional symbol of constancy

155 for 'em: that they do

157 green-sward: grass

158 smacks: suggests

160 blood look out: blush
good sooth: by God's truth

161 queen of curds and cream: Camillo expresses a similar judgement to that of Florizel at line 146 above, the curds and cream suggesting the sheep-shearing feast and the Arcadian world of which it seems to be part

162 strike up: start the music!

163–164 garlic...with: give her garlic to 'improve' her bad breath and thus her kisses

165 Now, in good time: – like 'marry' in the previous speech this exclamation is defined by its context and tone of delivery

166 stand upon: value

- *What significant word is used by both Florizel and Camillo to describe Perdita? How does Polixenes echo this recognition of her qualities?*

	And own no other function. Each your doing,	
	So singular in each particular,	
	Crowns what you are doing, in the present	
	deeds,	145
	That all your acts are queens.	

PERDITA   O Doricles,
Your praises are too large: but that your youth,
And the true blood which peeps fairly through 't,
Do plainly give you out an unstained shepherd,
With wisdom I might fear, my Doricles,   150
You wooed me the false way.

FLORIZEL   I think you have
As little skill to fear as I have purpose
To put you to 't. But come, our dance, I pray;
Your hand, my Perdita: so turtles pair
That never mean to part.

PERDITA   I'll swear for 'em.   155

POLIXENES   This is the prettiest low-born lass that ever
Ran on the green-sward: nothing she does or seems
But smacks of something greater than herself,
Too noble for this place.

CAMILLO   He tells her something
That makes her blood look out: good sooth,
she is   160
The queen of curds and cream.

CLOWN   Come on, strike up!

DORCAS   Mopsa must be your mistress: marry, garlic to
mend her kissing with!

MOPSA   Now, in good time!   165

CLOWN   Not a word, a word; we stand upon our manners.
Come, strike up!

     [*Music*] *Here a dance of* SHEPHERDS *and*
SHEPHERDESSES

POLIXENES   Pray, good shepherd, what fair swain is this

While the rustics dance, Polixenes asks about Florizel. The
Shepherd talks of Florizel's love for Perdita and hints at her
secret past. A servant announces the arrival of a pedlar. He
gives an account of the pedlar's vulgar songs.

171 a worthy feeding: valuable grazing land

173 like sooth: honest

174–176 never gazed...eyes: just as the moon gazes at the sea,
so he'll stand and gaze into my daughter's eyes. There are
references here to the moon as a symbol of chastity, of
womanhood and of madness. The image of the lover
reflected in the eyes of his beloved is also conventional.

177–178 not half a kiss...best: since it takes two to kiss, this is
a nice way of describing their mutual love

178 another: the other
featly: with graceful agility

181 light upon: settle upon, choose. 'To light on one's feet'
meant to be fortunate or successful. The line also suggests
what might result from Florizel lighting upon Perdita to
make love.

184 tabor: drum

186 tell: count

187 as: as if
ballads: ballads were doggerel verses on topical subjects
sung to popular folk tunes (see below, lines 263 ff.)

188 grew to: were captivated by

190 doleful: sad

191 pleasant: humorous

192 lamentably: like a lament, mournfully

196 bawdry: vulgarity

196–197 delicate burdens: delightful choruses

197 dildoes: the word occurs in the refrains of many songs of
the period but since it means an artificial penis it is always
vulgar or suggestive, as is 'jump her and thump her'
fadings: the refrain of another indecent popular song

198–201 stretch-mouthed rascal...good man: the servant is
apparently describing a song in which a loud-mouthed
young man is put off by the repeated cry of the girl

199–200 break a foul gap into the matter: never satisfactorily
explained but possibly a euphemism for the taking of
virginity

	Which dances with your daughter?
SHEPHERD	They call him Doricles; and boasts himself 170
	To have a worthy feeding: but I have it
	Upon his own report and I believe it;
	He looks like sooth. He says he loves my daughter:
	I think so too; for never gazed the moon
	Upon the water as he'll stand and read 175
	As 'twere my daughter's eyes: and, to be plain,
	I think there is not half a kiss to choose
	Who loves another best.
POLIXENES	She dances featly.
SHEPHERD	So she does anything, though I report it
	That should be silent. If young Doricles 180
	Do light upon her, she shall bring him that
	Which he not dreams of.

Enter SERVANT

SERVANT   O master! if you did but hear the pedlar at the
door, you would never dance again after a tabor
and pipe; no, the bagpipe could not move you: 185
he sings several tunes, faster than you'll tell money;
he utters them as he had eaten ballads, and all
men's ears grew to his tunes.

CLOWN   He could never come better: he shall come in. I
love a ballad but even too well, if it be doleful 190
matter merrily set down; or a very pleasant thing
indeed, and sung lamentably.

SERVANT   He hath songs for man or woman, of all sizes: no
milliner can so fit his customers with gloves: he has
the prettiest love-songs for maids, so without 195
bawdry (which is strange); with such delicate
burdens of dildoes and fadings, jump her and
thump her; and where some stretch-mouthed rascal
would, as it were, mean mischief and break a foul
gap into the matter, he makes the maid to 200
answer 'Whoop, do me no harm, good man;' puts

The servant describes the haberdashery in the pedlar's pack.
The Clown sends the servant to invite him in. It is, of course,
Autolycus who enters, singing his wares.

204 brave: admirable (ironic)
205–206 admirable conceited: remarkably ingenious
206 unbraided: new, not shop-soiled
208 points: laces to fasten clothing; arguments
209–210 by th' gross: wholesale; twelve dozen at a time
210 inkles, caddisses, cambrics, lawns: linen and worsted
   tapes, fine linen from Cambrai and Laon
211 sings 'em over: see Autolycus' song, below
213 sleeve-hand: cuff
213–214 work about the square on 't: the embroidery on the
   breast of it
219 You have of: some of
221 go about to: wish to
   Stage direction *Enter AUTOLYCUS*: Autolycus must be in
   disguise. It is likely that his main device is a false beard (see
   below, line 724).
223 Cypress: black cloth for mourning
224 Gloves as sweet: that is, having been perfumed, as was the
   fashion
225 Masks: since the fashion was for pale complexions, ladies
   often covered all or part of the face. Masks were also used to
   cover the ravages of syphilis.
226 Bugle: black bead
228 quoifs and stomachers: tightly-fitting ladies' caps and
   embroidered or bejewelled panels for dresses
230 poking-sticks: heated rods used to iron starched ruffs

	him off, slights him, with 'Whoop, do me no harm, good man.'	
POLIXENES	This is a brave fellow.	
CLOWN	Believe me, thou talkest of an admirable conceited fellow. Has he any unbraided wares?	205
SERVANT	He hath ribbons of all the colours i' th' rainbow; points, more than all the lawyers in Bohemia can learnedly handle, though they come to him by th' gross; inkles, caddisses, cambrics, lawns: why, he sings 'em over as they were gods or goddesses; you would think a smock were a she-angel, he so chants to the sleeve-hand and the work about the square on 't.	210
CLOWN	Prithee bring him in; and let him approach singing.	215
PERDITA	Forewarn him, that he use no scurrilous words in 's tunes. [*Exit* SERVANT	
CLOWN	You have of these pedlars that have more in them than you'd think, sister.	220
PERDITA	Ay, good brother, or go about to think.	

Enter AUTOLYCUS, *singing*

Lawn as white as driven snow,
Cypress black as e'er was crow,
Gloves as sweet as damask roses,
Masks for faces and for noses: 225
Bugle-bracelet, necklace amber,
Perfume for a lady's chamber:
Golden quoifs and stomachers
For my lads to give their dears:
Pins, and poking-sticks of steel,   230
What maids lack from head to heel:
Come buy of me, come! come buy! come buy!
Buy, lads, or else your lasses cry.
Come buy!

Mopsa and Dorcas argue over the Clown and the gifts he
was supposed to buy them. He reminds them that he was
cheated of his money but fails to recognize Autolycus as the
trickster.

237 **bondage**: parcelling up
239 **against**: before
247 **wear their plackets**: literally, 'display their petticoats', but
     the placket was also the pocket in a skirt and thus a
     euphemism for vagina. Here it follows naturally from
     Mopsa's insinuations about the sexual favours that the
     Clown has 'promised' Dorcas and perhaps 'paid' her.
249 **kiln-hole**: the fire-hole of a kiln; in the kitchen
     whistle: whisper
251 **clamor**: silence
253 **tawdry-lace**: brightly-coloured scarf; 'tawdry' is a
     contraction of Saint Audrey on whose saint's day a fair was
     held at Ely
255–256 **cozened by the way**: cheated on the road
260–261 **parcels of charge**: goods of value
263 **a life**: on my life
266 **usurer**: money-lender
     was brought to bed of: gave birth to
267 **at a burden**: at the same time
268 **carbonadoed**: cut up, scored across and grilled

> • *Consider the relationship between the Clown and the*
>   *Shepherdesses. What aspects of the relationship between*
>   *Florizel and Perdita do they serve to highlight?*

CLOWN   If I were not in love with Mopsa, thou shouldst 235
         take no money of me; but being enthralled as I am,
         it will also be the bondage of certain ribbons and
         gloves.

MOPSA   I was promised them against the feast; but they
         come not too late now.   240

DORCAS   He hath promised you more than that, or there be
         liars.

MOPSA   He hath paid you all he promised you: may be he
         has paid you more, which will shame you to give
         him again.   245

CLOWN   Is there no manners left among maids? Will they
         wear their plackets where they should bear
         their faces? Is there not milking-time, when you are
         going to bed, or kiln-hole, to whistle of these
         secrets, but you must be tittle-tattling before all 250
         our guests? 'Tis well they are whispering: clamor
         your tongues, and not a word more.

MOPSA   I have done. Come, you promised me a tawdry-lace
         and a pair of sweet gloves.

CLOWN   Have I not told thee how I was cozened by the 255
         way and lost all my money?

AUTOLYCUS And indeed, sir, there are cozeners abroad;
         therefore it behoves men to be wary.

CLOWN   Fear not thou, man, thou shalt lose nothing here.

AUTOLYCUS I hope so, sir; for I have about me many parcels 260
         of charge.

CLOWN   What hast here? Ballads?

MOPSA   Pray now, buy some: I love a ballad in print, a life,
         for then we are sure they are true.

AUTOLYCUS Here's one, to a very doleful tune, how a   265
         usurer's wife was brought to bed of twenty money-
         bags at a burden, and how she longed to eat adders'
         heads and toads carbonadoed.

Autolycus advertises his ballads and the Clown, Mopsa and
Dorcas, believing every word, reveal their naiveté.

276 moe: more
278 another ballad of a fish: many such ballads existed but
Autolycus exaggerates absurdly. The audience will laugh at both
his satire of ballads and Dorcas' credulity.
283 exchange: interchange, hence another euphemism for sexual
intercourse
286 hands: signatures
292 Two maids wooing a man: no ballad of this title survives but
the words of 'Get you hence' (lines 300–315 below) are known
to have been part of a popular contemporary song which may
have existed before Shakespeare used it here, and they clearly fit
the title. When Mopsa says 'We can both sing it' she means
'Two maids wooing a man', which they have learned by heart,
and not the 'merry one' which Autolycus claims to be selling
but which the women would be unable to sing at sight. Mopsa
and Dorcas are keen to show that they are no less sophisticated
than the maids 'westward'.
295 bear a part: sing independently a line of music in a part-song
299 have at it: I'll try it

- *Suggest some contemporary parallels to Autolycus' ballads.*

MOPSA	Is it true, think you?
AUTOLYCUS	Very true, and but a month old. 270
DORCAS	Bless me from marrying a usurer!
AUTOLYCUS	Here's the midwife's name to 't, one Mistress Taleporter, and five or six honest wives that were present. Why should I carry lies abroad?
MOPSA	[*To* CLOWN] Pray you now, buy it. 275
CLOWN	Come on, lay it by: and let's first see moe ballads: we'll buy the other things anon.
AUTOLYCUS	Here's another ballad of a fish that appeared upon the coast on Wednesday the fourscore of April, forty thousand fathom above water, and sung 280 this ballad against the hard hearts of maids: it was thought she was a woman, and was turned into a cold fish for she would not exchange flesh with one that loved her. The ballad is very pitiful, and as true.
DORCAS	Is it true too, think you? 285
AUTOLYCUS	Five justices' hands at it, and witnesses more than my pack will hold.
CLOWN	Lay it by too: another.
AUTOLYCUS	This is a merry ballad, but a very pretty one.
MOPSA	Let's have some merry ones. 290
AUTOLYCUS	Why, this is a passing merry one and goes to the tune of 'Two maids wooing a man:' there's scarce a maid westward but she sings it; 'tis in request, I can tell you.
MOPSA	We can both sing it: if thou'lt bear a part, thou 295 shalt hear; 'tis in three parts.
DORCAS	We had the tune on 't a month ago.
AUTOLYCUS	I can bear my part; you must know 'tis my occupation: have at it with you: [*Song*]

Autolycus, Mopsa and Dorcas sing the part-song 'Get you hence'. Meanwhile the Shepherd and Polixenes continue in serious conversation. The Clown ushers the singers out of their hearing.

308 grange: country house and farm buildings
317 sad: serious
326 toys: trifling ornaments
329–330 Money's a meddler...ware-a: money has a hand in everything and is the currency for all men's goods

• *Look at the Clown's speech. What might he be feeling that motivates these words? What stage business might have accompanied the song?*

AUTOLYCUS	Get you hence, for I must go	300
	Where it fits not you to know.	
DORCAS	Whither?	
MOPSA	O whither?	
DORCAS	Whither?	
MOPSA	It becomes thy oath full well,	305
	Thou to me thy secrets tell:	
DORCAS	Me too: let me go thither.	
MOPSA	Or thou goest to th' grange or mill:	
DORCAS	If to either, thou dost ill.	
AUTOLYCUS	Neither.	310
DORCAS	What neither?	
AUTOLYCUS	Neither.	
DORCAS	Thou hast sworn my love to be;	
MOPSA	Thou hast sworn it more to me:	
	Then whither goest? Say whither?	315

CLOWN We'll have this song out anon by ourselves: my
father and the gentlemen are in sad talk, and we'll
not trouble them. Come, bring away thy pack after
me. Wenches, I'll buy for you both. Pedlar,
let's have the first choice. Follow me, girls.   320
                    [*Exit with* DORCAS *and* MOPSA

AUTOLYCUS And you shall pay well for 'em.

[*Song*]
          Will you buy any tape,
          Or lace for your cape,
          My dainty duck, my dear-a?
          Any silk, any thread,   325
          Any toys for your head,
          Of the new'st, and fin'st, fin'st wear-a?
          Come to the pedlar;
          Money's a meddler,
          That doth utter all men's ware-a.   [*Exit* 330

As Autolycus exits the servant announces the arrival of twelve rustic dancers to perform a gymnastic satyr dance. As the dance finishes Polixenes concludes his conversation with the Shepherd and, having decided that it is time to part Perdita and Florizel, speaks to his son.

332 neat-herds: cowherds

333 all men of hair: the dancers were dressed in skins to represent the satyrs of Greek legend: half man, half goat, minor woodland gods and noted for their sexual excesses

334 Saltiers: the servant's mispronunciation of satyr. Salt or sault meant jump as in somersault.

335 gallimaufry of gambols: chaotic medley of running and jumping. Such a satyr dance (in Ben Jonson's masque *Oberon*) is known to have been performed before the royal court in 1611 and it has been suggested that Shakespeare's company was here taking the opportunity to perform on the public stage an act which had already been a private success (see below, lines 344–345).

338 bowling: the contrast is with a quiet country game, but the servant may also be referring to sexual behaviour

346–347 by th' square: precisely; according to exact measurement

348 Leave your prating: cease your chatter

351 O, father...hereafter: the conclusion to the 'sad talk' which has continued despite the song and dance (see line 317 and the next note)

353 simple: innocent, humble, of low degree; 'stupid' is generally a later meaning so Polixenes is not referring to Florizel but to the Old Shepherd who has been describing the courtship of Florizel and Perdita

356 handed: dealt with, was engaged in

357 knacks: trifles (see toys, line 326)

Enter SERVANT

SERVANT   Master, there is three carters, three shepherds,
                 three neat-herds, three swine-herds, that have made
                 themselves all men of hair. They call themselves
                 Saltiers, and they have a dance which the wenches
                 say is a gallimaufry of gambols, because they are 335
                 not in 't: but they themselves are o' the mind (if it
                 be not too rough for some that know little but
                 bowling) it will please plentifully.

SHEPHERD   Away! we'll none on 't: here has been too much
                 homely foolery already. I know, sir, we weary   340
                 you.

POLIXENES   You weary those that refresh us: pray, let's see these
                 four threes of herdsmen.

SERVANTS   One three of them, by their own report, sir, hath
                 danced before the king; and not the worst of   345
                 the three but jumps twelve foot and a half by
                 th' square.

SHEPHERD   Leave your prating: since these good men are
                 pleased, let them come in; but quickly now.

SERVANTS   Why, they stay at door, sir.   350

Here a dance of twelve Satyrs.

POLIXENES   O, father, you'll know more of that hereafter.
                 [*To* CAMILLO] Is it not too far gone? 'Tis time to
                     part them.
                 He's simple and tells much. [*To* FLORIZEL] How
                     now, fair shepherd!
                 Your heart is full of something that does take
                 Your mind from feasting. Sooth, when I was
                     young   355
                 And handed love, as you do, I was wont
                 To load my she with knacks: I would have
                     ransacked
                 The pedlar's silken treasury, and have poured it

Polixenes questions his son (who still does not recognize him) about his relationship with Perdita. Florizel begins a public proclamation of his love.

360 nothing marted: done no trade
361 Interpretation should abuse: should misinterpret
362 bounty: generosity
  straited: in great difficulty
363–364 if you make...her: if you care for her continued happiness and love
366 looks: expects
368–369 O hear me...sir: (to Perdita) hear me make vows of lifelong love in front of this elderly, honourable man (Polixenes)
372 Ethiopian: synonymous with Negro and the epitome of blackness, against which the teeth would show most white
  bolted: sifted
375 was: which was
  put you out: put you off; distracted you
378 this my neighbour: that is, Camillo
382 force: strength

	To her acceptance: you have let him go,	
	And nothing marted with him. If your lass	360
	Interpretation should abuse, and call this	
	Your lack of love or bounty, you were straited	
	For a reply, at least if you make a care	
	Of happy holding her.	

FLORIZEL   Old sir, I know

She prizes not such trifles as these are: 365
The gifts she looks from me are packed and locked
Up in my heart, which I have given already,
But not delivered. [*To* PERDITA] O hear me breathe
   my life
Before this ancient sir, who, it should seem,
Hath sometime loved. I take thy hand, this
   hand,   370
As soft as dove's down and as white as it,
Or Ethiopian's tooth, or the fanned snow that's
   bolted
By th' northern blasts twice o'er.

POLIXENES   What follows this?

How prettily the young swain seems to wash
The hand was fair before! I have put you out: 375
But to your protestation: let me hear
What you profess.

FLORIZEL   Do, and be witness to 't.

POLIXENES   And this my neighbour too?

FLORIZEL   And he, and more

Than he, and men, the earth, the heavens, and
   all;
That were I crowned the most imperial
   monarch   380
Thereof most worthy, were I the fairest youth
That ever made eye swerve, had force and
   knowledge
More than was ever man's, I would not prize
   them

Florizel and Perdita declare their love. The Shepherd offers
Perdita a dowry equal to that of Florizel. He promises that
he will one day inherit much more than they can imagine.
He asks Polixenes and Camillo to witness the betrothal but
Polixenes wants to know about Florizel's father.

385–386 Commend them...perdition: commend them to her
    service or condemn them to hell; a 'retrospective
    construction' – compare Act 3 scene 2 lines 163–165
390–391 By th' pattern...his: our thoughts are identical. The
    metaphor, from cutting cloth to a pattern, suits a shepherd's
    daughter
394 portion: dowry
395 one: that is, Polixenes
396 yet: at present

> - *How is irony used to increase the dramatic tension
>   here?*

	Without her love; for her, employ them all;
	Commend them and condemn them to her
	service, 385
	Or to their own perdition.
POLIXENES	Fairly offered.
CAMILLO	This shows a sound affection.
SHEPHERD	But my daughter,
	Say you the like to him?
PERDITA	I cannot speak
	So well, nothing so well; no, nor mean better:
	By th' pattern of mine own thoughts I cut out 390
	The purity of his.
SHEPHERD	Take hands, a bargain!
	And, friends unknown, you shall bear witness to 't.
	I give my daughter to him, and will make
	Her portion equal his.
FLORIZEL	O, that must be
	I' th' virtue of your daughter: one being dead, 395
	I shall have more than you can dream of yet;
	Enough then for your wonder. But come on,
	Contract us 'fore these witnesses.
SHEPHERD	Come, your hand;
	And, daughter, yours.
POLIXENES	Soft, swain, awhile, beseech you;
	Have you a father?
FLORIZEL	I have: but what of him? 400
POLIXENES	Knows he of this?
FLORIZEL	He neither does nor shall.
POLIXENES	Methinks a father
	Is at the nuptial of his son a guest
	That best becomes the table. Pray you once
	more,
	Is not your father grown incapable 405
	Of reasonable affairs? Is he not stupid

Florizel refuses to tell his father of his betrothal. Polixenes attempts to persuade him but the young man is adamant. They argue with increasing vehemence. Polixenes removes his disguise, threatens his son with disinheritance and the Old Shepherd with death.

407 alt'ring rheums: secretions from the mouth, eyes or nose which have changed him from what he was. Rheums, when excessive, were taken as a sign of disease.

408 Dispute his own estate: discuss his own affairs

414–418 reason my son...business: it is reasonable that my son should choose himself a wife but it is just as reasonable that the father, whose happiness is entirely in ensuring his family's future, should be able to advise on the matter. Polixenes' use of 'my son' is ambiguous and ironic: he is being hypothetical but also addressing Florizel in a friendly fashion.

425 Mark: observe

contract: betrothal which, depending on the form Florizel intended to use, could be legally binding. Polixenes' use of the words 'nuptial' in line 403 and 'divorce' in this line suggest that he at least sees Florizel's action as irrevocable.

Mark: pay attention to; consider

428 affects: aspires to, desires (see below, line 489)

sheep-hook: shepherd's crook – the symbol of the shepherd's role, just as 'sceptre' in the previous line is symbolic of kingship

With age and alt'ring rheums? Can he speak, hear,
Know man from man? Dispute his own estate?
Lies he not bed-rid and again does nothing
But what he did being childish?

FLORIZEL   No, good sir;   410
He has his health, and ampler strength indeed
Than most have of his age.

POLIXENES   By my white beard,
You offer him, if this be so, a wrong
Something unfilial: reason my son
Should choose himself a wife, but as good
        reason   415
The father (all whose joy is nothing else
But fair posterity) should hold some counsel
In such a business.

FLORIZEL   I yield all this;
But for some other reasons, my grave sir,
Which 'tis not fit you know, I not acquaint   420
My father of this business.

POLIXENES   Let him know 't.

FLORIZEL   He shall not.

POLIXENES   Prithee, let him.

FLORIZEL   No, he must not.

SHEPHERD   Let him, my son: he shall not need to grieve
At knowing of thy choice.

FLORIZEL   Come, come, he must not.
Mark our contract.

POLIXENES   Mark your divorce, young sir, 425
                        [*Discovering himself*
Whom son I dare not call; thou art too base
To be acknowledged: thou a sceptre's heir,
That thus affects a sheep-hook! Thou, old traitor,
I am sorry that by hanging thee I can
But shorten thy life one week. And thou, fresh
        piece   430

Polixenes threatens Perdita with torture. As he exits Perdita
reveals that her fears of discovery have been realized. She
invites Florizel to leave.

431 of force: of course

432 thou cop'st with: you are engaged with; in this context the
phrase has overtones of sexual contact

434 More homely...state: more unattractive than your social
position
fond: foolish

436 knack: worthless thing

437 we'll: as monarch and embodiment of the state, Polixenes
refers to himself in the plural

439 Farre than Deucalion off: *farre* is an older form of
'farther', the comparative of 'far' – Deucalion was the
Ancient Greek equivalent of Noah and thus notionally the
ancestor of all humanity; Polixenes' hyperbole thus
disinherits his son from the human race

440 Thou churl: you peasant (the Shepherd)

442 enchantment: Perdita, the 'fresh piece of excellent
witchcraft' (lines 430–431)

443–445 yea, him too...thee: yes, even (worthy) of him who
would have made himself unworthy of you had it not been
for my royal blood in him.

456 state: condition; but a further sense, royal position, suggests
Perdita's play on 'queen' in the next line (compare lines 5,
146 and 161 above)

459 Speak ere thou diest: Polixenes has reprieved the Shepherd
(lines 440–442) but Shakespeare has further melodrama to
derive from the sentence, so Camillo's teasing words are
accepted on face value by the gullible Shepherd here and
later in the scene.

- *What imagery does Polixenes use in describing
  Perdita? In what ways does his language contrast with
  his previous observations?*

Of excellent witchcraft, who, of force, must know
The royal fool thou cop'st with, –

SHEPHERD   O, my heart!

POLIXENES I'll have thy beauty scratched with briers and made
More homely than thy state. For thee, fond boy,
If I may ever know thou dost but sigh   435
That thou no more shalt see this knack (as never
I mean thou shalt), we'll bar thee from succession;
Not hold thee of our blood, no, not our kin,
Farre than Deucalion off. Mark thou my words!
Follow us to the court. Thou churl, for this
    time,   440
Though full of our displeasure, yet we free thee
From the dead blow of it. And you,
    enchantment, –
Worthy enough a herdsman; yea, him too,
That makes himself, but for our honour therein,
Unworthy thee. If ever henceforth thou   445
These rural latches to his entrance open,
Or hoop his body more with thy embraces,
I will devise a death as cruel for thee
As thou art tender to 't.   [*Exit*

PERDITA   Even here, undone,
I was not much afeard; for once or twice   450
I was about to speak, and tell him plainly,
The selfsame sun that shines upon his court
Hides not his visage from our cottage, but
Looks on alike. Will't please you, sir, be gone?
I told you what would come of this: beseech
    you,   455
Of your own state take care: this dream of mine –
Being now awake, I'll queen it no inch farther,
But milk my ewes, and weep.

CAMILLO   [*To* OLD SHEPHERD] Why, how now,
    father!
Speak ere thou diest.

The Shepherd blames Perdita for the disaster and exits.
Florizel says that he still intends to marry Perdita but
Camillo advises him to avoid Polixenes until the King has
calmed down. Camillo removes his disguise.

466 Where no priest shovels in dust: that is, in unconsecrated
ground beneath the gallows

469–470 I have lived...desire: I should have lived as long as I
would wish

473–474 More straining...unwillingly: like a hound, the more
I am held back the more I strain forward; I am not being led
unwillingly (towards marriage)

481 Camillo?: presumably the cue for Camillo to remove his
disguise

483 dignity: high rank; the word is the subject of ' 'twere' and
'It' in the next line

486–487 Let nature...within: the image is of all earthly life
growing from seeds inside the pod or womb of the Earth.
The vehement magnitude of Florizel's image is akin to his
father's (lines **438–439**) to which he now, in the next line,
responds.

> • *In reply to Camillo the Shepherd speaks with a dignity
> which reflects the courtier's own. He even echoes
> Camillo's words (Act 1 scene 2 line 376).*

SHEPHERD   I cannot speak, nor think,
                    Nore dare to know that which I know. O sir!   460
                    You have undone a man of fourscore three,
                    That thought to fill his grave in quiet; yea,
                    To die upon the bed my father died,
                    To lie close by his honest bones: but now
                    Some hangman must put on my shroud and lay
                        me   465
                    Where no priest shovels in dust. O cursed wretch,
                    That knew'st this was the prince, and wouldst
                        adventure
                    To mingle faith with him! Undone! undone!
                    If I might die within this hour, I have lived
                    To die when I desire.   [*Exit*

FLORIZEL   Why look you so upon me?   470
                    I am but sorry, not afeard; delayed,
                    But nothing altered: what I was, I am;
                    More straining on for plucking back; not following
                    My leash unwillingly.

CAMILLO   Gracious my lord,
                    You know your father's temper: at this time   475
                    He will allow no speech (which, I do guess,
                    You do not purpose to him) and as hardly
                    Will he endure your sight as yet, I fear:
                    Then, till the fury of his highness settle,
                    Come not before him.

FLORIZEL   I not purpose it.   480
                    I think – Camillo?

CAMILLO   Even he, my lord.

PERDITA   How often have I told you 'twould be thus!
                    How often said, my dignity would last
                    But till 'twere known!

FLORIZEL   It cannot fail, but by
                    The violation of my faith; and then   485
                    Let nature crush the sides o' th' earth together,

Despite Camillo's advice Florizel is adamant that he will
marry Perdita. He asks Camillo to intercede with his father
but meanwhile plans to take Perdita on board his ship and
leave the country.

489 Am heir to my affection: see 'affects' above, line 428

490 fancy: love

490–493 If my reason...welcome: if my reason will be
obedient to my love I shall remain sane; otherwise my
feelings, which prefer unreason, will bid love welcome

496–497 nor the pomp...gleaned: nor for the splendid display
that may be had there. To glean is to pick up the ears of
corn which have been left by the reapers; Florizel's use of
the word implies the small value he places upon pomp.

498 The close earth wombs: see above, lines 486–487 and note

504–505 let myself...come: let chance and me fight for my
future

511–512 Shall nothing benefit...reporting: there is no value
in your knowing nor is it my business to tell you

513 were easier for: would more easily take

515 by and by: soon

irremoveable: stubborn; immoveable

	And mar the seeds within! Lift up thy looks:
	From my succession wipe me, father; I
	Am heir to my affection.
CAMILLO	Be advised.
FLORIZEL	I am, and by my fancy. If my reason 490
	Will thereto be obedient, I have reason;
	If not, my senses, better pleased with madness,
	Do bid it welcome.
CAMILLO	This is desperate, sir.
FLORIZEL	So call it, but it does fulfil my vow;
	I needs must think it honesty. Camillo, 495
	Not for Bohemia, nor the pomp that may
	Be thereat gleaned: for all the sun sees, or
	The close earth wombs, or the profound seas hides
	In unknown fathoms, will I break my oath
	To this my fair beloved. Therefore, I pray you, 500
	As you have ever been my father's honoured friend,
	When he shall miss me, – as, in faith, I mean not
	To see him any more, – cast your good counsels
	Upon his passion: let myself and fortune
	Tug for the time to come. This you may know, 505
	And so deliver: I am put to sea
	With her whom here I cannot hold on shore;
	And most opportune to our need, I have
	A vessel rides fast by, but not prepared
	For this design. What course I mean to hold 510
	Shall nothing benefit your knowledge, nor
	Concern me the reporting.
CAMILLO	O my lord,
	I would your spirit were easier for advice,
	Or stronger for your need.
FLORIZEL	Hark, Perdita.
	[*To* CAMILLO] I'll hear you by and by.
CAMILLO	He's irremoveable, 515
	Resolved for flight. Now were I happy, if

In a soliloquy Camillo tells the audience that he plans to help Florizel whilst also creating the opportunity to visit Sicilia. He advises the Prince that he can guide him to a safe destination where he will be assured of an appropriate welcome.

522 curious: worrying; unfamiliar

527–528 not little...on: he tries hard to reward your deeds as soon (and as fully) as he is aware of them

532 ponderous and settled: weighty and established; Camillo is not so much being sarcastic as playing the role of courtier and diplomat for which Florizel has just praised him

535 become your highness: be appropriate to one of your rank

537 disjunction: separation

540 discontenting: angry
   qualify: appease

544 after that: in accordance with your more-than-human abilities

> • *There have been a number of revelations in this scene but what deceptions and disguises remain?*

His going I could frame to serve my turn,
Save him from danger, do him love and
    honour,
Purchase the sight again of dear Sicilia
And that unhappy king, my master, whom   520
I so much thirst to see.

FLORIZEL   Now good Camillo;
I am so fraught with curious business that
I leave out ceremony.

CAMILLO   Sir, I think
You have heard of my poor services, i' th' love
That I have borne your father?

FLORIZEL   Very nobly   525
Have you deserved: it is my father's music
To speak your deeds, not little of his care
To have them recompensed as thought on.

CAMILLO   Well, my lord,
If you may please to think I love the king,
And through him what's nearest to him, which
    is   530
Your gracious self, embrace but my direction,
If your more ponderous and settled project
May suffer alteration. On mine honour,
I'll point you where you shall have such receiving
As shall become your highness; where you may 535
Enjoy your mistress; from the whom, I see,
There's no disjunction to be made, but by –
As heavens forefend! – your ruin. Marry her,
And with my best endeavours in your absence
Your discontenting father strive to qualify   540
And bring him up to liking.

FLORIZEL   How, Camillo,
May this, almost a miracle, be done? –
That I may call thee something more than man
And after that trust to thee.

Camillo advises Florizel to take Perdita to Sicilia where he is confident that the penitent Leontes will welcome them with open arms. Florizel wants a good reason for his visit there. Camillo promises to write down all that Florizel must say in order to seem a credible ambassador from his father.

546–547 But as th' unthought-on...do: but as an unexpected chance event is to blame for our unplanned action

548–549 flies Of every wind that blows: compare Leontes, Act 2 scene 3 line 153

554 habited: dressed

556 free: generous, noble

557 asks thee there, 'Son: some editors follow the *Third Folio* in emending this to 'asks thee, the son' but this is unnecessary since Camillo's imagined direct speech is more dramatic and, at this critical moment, more likely to persuade Florizel

558 As 'twere...person: as if he had the father himself (to ask forgiveness of)

559 fresh: young, lovely

560 his unkindness and his kindness: that is, unkindness towards Polixenes and the kindness with which he intends to treat Florizel and Perdita

561 chides: scolds

563 colour: reason, pretext

566–572 with What you...heart: Camillo says he will write details of events in Sicilia which could only have been known to Leontes, Polixenes and Camillo. Leontes will thus believe that everything said by Florizel comes from Polixenes' heart.

- *If Camillo's suggested plan is adhered to, how would you expect the play to end?*

CAMILLO   Have you thought on
         A place whereto you'll go?

FLORIZEL   Not any yet: 545
         But as th' unthought-on accident is guilty
         To what we wildly do, so we profess
         Ourselves to be the slaves of chance, and flies
         Of every wind that blows.

CAMILLO   Then list to me:
         This follows, if you will not change your
                 purpose,   550
         But undergo this flight; make for Sicilia,
         And there present yourself and your fair princess
         (For so I see she must be) 'fore Leontes:
         She shall be habited as it becomes
         The partner of your bed. Methinks I see   555
         Leontes opening his free arms and weeping
         His welcomes forth; asks thee there, 'Son,
                 forgiveness!'
         As 'twere i' th' father's person; kisses the hands
         Of your fresh princess; o'er and o'er divides him
         'Twixt his unkindness and his kindness; th' one 560
         He chides to hell, and bids the other grow
         Faster than thought or time.

FLORIZEL   Worthy Camillo,
         What colour for my visitation shall I
         Hold up before him?

CAMILLO   Sent by the king your father
         To greet him and to give him comforts. Sir,   565
         The manner of your bearing towards him, with
         What you (as from your father) shall deliver,
         Things known betwixt us three, I'll write you down:
         The which shall point you forth at every sitting
         What you must say; that he shall not perceive   570
         But that you have your father's bosom there
         And speak his very heart.

FLORIZEL   I am bound to you:

Camillo convinces the young couple that any other course of action would be too hazardous. Perdita will not accept that suffering could alter her love for Florizel. The prince and the courtier both compliment her.

573 sap: life

578–580 Nothing so certain...be: such a course would be less predictable even than your anchors, and their only purpose is to stop you drifting from bad to worse

581–583 Prosperity's the...Affliction alters: good fortune binds lovers together but their appearance of good health and love for each other are both changed for the worse by suffering

586 these seven years: proverbial expression meaning 'for a very long time'

588–589 She is as forward...birth: she is as far above her upbringing as she is below me in her birth – an example of dramatic irony

593 the thorns we stand upon: proverbial expression indicating impatient anxiety

596 furnished: equipped

597 appear: appear to be (his son)

There is some sap in this.

CAMILLO   A course more promising
Than a wild dedication of yourselves
To unpathed waters, undreamed shores; most
    certain   575
To miseries enough: no hope to help you,
But as you shake off one, to take another:
Nothing so certain as your anchors, who
Do their best office if they can but stay you
Where you'll be loath to be. Besides, you know 580
Prosperity's the very bond of love,
Whose fresh complexion and whose heart
    together
Affliction alters.

PERDITA   One of these is true:
I think affliction may subdue the cheek,
But not take in the mind.

CAMILLO   Yea? say you so?   585
There shall not, at your father's house, these seven
    years
Be born another such.

FLORIZEL   My good Camillo
She is as forward of her breeding as
She is i' th' rear 'our birth.

CAMILLO   I cannot say 'tis pity
She lacks instructions, for she seems a mistress 590
To most that teach.

PERDITA   Your pardon, sir; for this
I'll blush you thanks.

FLORIZEL   My prettiest Perdita!
But O, the thorns we stand upon! Camillo,
Preserver of my father, now of me,
The medicine of our house, how shall we do?   595
We are not furnished like Bohemia's son,
Nor shall appear in Sicilia.

Camillo promises to pay Florizel's expenses from his Sicilian wealth. As they discuss details Autolycus enters. He is rejoicing that not only has he sold all his pedlar's wares but he has picked the pockets of anyone with money.

600 royally appointed: equipped in the manner of royalty

600–601 as if The...mine: as if you were appearing in a stage play at my direction

603 Honesty, Trust: Autolycus personifies these virtues as if they were characters in a morality play; his imagery unconsciously echoes that of Camillo two lines earlier

605 trumpery: trash, worthless goods

606 pomander: perfumed sachet or bag which was carried to ward off infection

606 table-book: notebook

607–608 horn-ring: rings containing horn were supposed to have magical qualities

610 hallowed...benediction: sacred relics which brought a blessing

611–612 best in picture: an otherwise unknown usage but the sense seems to be 'best to look at' or 'most easily seen' (and thus picked)

616 pettitoes: literally, pig's trotters; suggested by the description of the Clown in the parentheses and leading to the use of 'herd' in the next line

618–619 pinched a placket: picked a pocket, stolen a virginity; see note to line 247 above

619–620 geld a codpiece: cut a purse from the flap-pocket at the front of a man's breeches; however, geld means castrate and codpiece is a euphemism for penis.

622 nothing: a pun on 'nothing' meaning triviality and 'noting', a tune

626 choughs: jackdaws, foolish birds

- *'...as if The scene you play were mine' (lines 600–601):* this is one of a number of reminders that we are, after all, only watching a play.

CAMILLO   My lord,
              Fear none of this. I think you know my fortunes
              Do all lie there: it shall be so my care
              To have you royally appointed, as if   600
              The scene you play were mine. For instance, sir,
              That you may know you shall not want, – one
                  word.

                                            [*They talk aside*

              Enter AUTOLYCUS

AUTOLYCUS   Ha, ha! What a fool Honesty is, and Trust, his
              sworn brother, a very simple gentleman! I have sold
              all my trumpery: not a counterfeit stone, not a   605
              ribbon, glass, pomander, brooch, table-book,
              ballad, knife, tape, glove, shoe-tie, bracelet, horn-
              ring, to keep my pack from fasting. They throng
              who should buy first, as if my trinkets had been
              hallowed and brought a benediction to the   610
              buyer: by which means I saw whose purse was best
              in picture; and what I saw, to my good use
              I remembered. My clown (who wants but
              something to be a reasonable man) grew so in love
              with the wenches' song, that he would not stir   615
              his pettitoes till he had both tune and words; which
              so drew the rest of the herd to me, that all their
              other senses stuck in ears. You might have pinched
              a placket, it was senseless; 'twas nothing to geld a
              codpiece of a purse; I would have filed keys off   620
              that hung in chains: no hearing, no feeling, but my
              sir's song, and admiring the nothing of it. So that
              in this time of lethargy I picked and cut most of
              their festival purses; and had not the old man come
              in with a hubbub against his daughter and the   625
              king's son, and scared my choughs from the chaff,
              I had not left a purse alive in the whole army.

                  [CAMILLO, FLORIZEL, *and* PERDITA *come forward*]

Camillo notices Autolycus and demands that he exchange
clothes with Florizel. Autolycus pleads poverty and is
rewarded. Autolycus and Florizel exchange clothes.

633 **make an instrument of this**: use this man
641 **discase thee**: undress
642 **think**: understand
643–644 **the pennyworth...worst**: though he gets the worst of
    the bargain
645 **boot**: further reward
646 **I know ye**: since he claimed to have been Florizel's servant
    (Act 4 scene 3 line 13)
648 **flayed**: skinned, undressed
653 **earnest**: part payment – a pun on his previous use of the
    word in line 650

> • *More disguises – throughout the play people are rarely
>   what they seem to be.*
> • *'I smell the trick on 't': Autolycus thinks he knows what
>   is happening, but how much does he know and of what
>   is he ignorant?*

CAMILLO	Nay, but my letters, by this means being there So soon as you arrive, shall clear that doubt.
FLORIZEL	And those that you'll procure from King Leontes? 630
CAMILLO	Shall satisfy your father.
PERDITA	Happy be you! All that you speak shows fair.
CAMILLO	[*Seeing* AUTOLYCUS] Who have we here? We'll make an instrument of this; omit Nothing may give us aid.
AUTOLYCUS	If they have overheard me now, – why, hanging. 635
CAMILLO	How now, good fellow! why shakest thou so? Fear not, man; here's no harm intended to thee.
AUTOLYCUS	I am a poor fellow, sir.
CAMILLO	Why, be so still; here's nobody will steal that from thee. Yet for the outside of thy poverty we must 640 make an exchange; therefore discase thee instantly, – thou must think there's a necessity in 't – and change garments with this gentleman. Though the pennyworth on his side be the worst, yet hold thee, there's some boot. 645
AUTOLYCUS	I am a poor fellow, sir. [*Aside*] I know ye well enough.
CAMILLO	Nay, prithee, dispatch: the gentleman is half flayed already.
AUTOLYCUS	Are you in earnest, sir? [*Aside*] I smell the trick 650 on 't.
FLORIZEL	Dispatch, I prithee.
AUTOLYCUS	Indeed, I have had earnest; but I cannot with conscience take it.
CAMILLO	Unbuckle, unbuckle. 655

[FLORIZEL *and* AUTOLYCUS *exchange garments*

Perdita is also disguised. In a soliloquy Camillo reveals that he will tell Polixenes of Florizel's escape in the hope that the King will go in pursuit of the young couple. Camillo will accompany him and thus return to Sicilia. Florizel, Perdita and Camillo exit, leaving Autolycus in a new disguise.

657 Come home to ye: come true for you – that is, the prophecy that she will be fortunate

660–661 Dismantle you...seeming: take off your cloak and disguise your appearance as well as you can; 'as you can' is perhaps a reminder that Perdita is still 'goddess-like pranked up'

662 eyes over: spies watching; see Act 4 scene 2 lines 36–37

663 undescried: unseen

663–664 I see the play...part: I see that this drama demands that I play a part in it

668 what have...forgot: we are never given the answer to the question which is essentially an opportunity for Camillo's soliloquy

675 a woman's longing: an emotional attachment, perhaps also with the suggestion that he will burst into tears at the sight of Sicilia

	Fortunate mistress, – let my prophecy	
	Come home to ye! – you must retire yourself	
	Into some covert: take your sweetheart's hat	
	And pluck it o'er your brows, muffle your face,	
	Dismantle you, and (as you can) disliken	660
	The truth of your own seeming; that you may	
	(For I do fear eyes over) to shipboard	
	Get undescried.	
PERDITA	I see the play so lies	
	That I must bear a part.	
CAMILLO	No remedy.	
	Have you done there?	
FLORIZEL	Should I now meet my father	665
	He would not call me son.	
CAMILLO	Nay, you shall have no hat.	
	[*Giving it to* PERDITA	
	Come, lady, come. Farewell, my friend.	
AUTOLYCUS	Adieu, sir.	
FLORIZEL	O Perdita, what have we twain forgot?	
	Pray you, a word. [*They draw aside*	
CAMILLO	What I do next, shall be to tell the king	670
	Of this escape and whither they are bound;	
	Wherein my hope is I shall so prevail	
	To force him after: in whose company	
	I shall re-view Sicilia, for whose sight	
	I have a woman's longing.	
FLORIZEL	Fortune speed us!	675
	Thus we set on, Camillo, to th' sea-side.	
CAMILLO	The swifter speed, the better.	

[*Exeunt* FLORIZEL, PERDITA, *and* CAMILLO

AUTOLYCUS	I understand the business, I hear it. To have an	
	open ear, a quick eye, and a nimble hand, is	
	necessary for a cut-purse; a good nose is	680
	requisite also, to smell out work for the other	

Autolycus meditates on his good fortune and decides to keep quiet about all that he has heard. The Clown and the Shepherd enter. The Clown tells his father to avoid punishment by revealing to the king the writings that he found with the baby and that Perdita is a changeling. The Shepherd agrees to go to the king.

684 What a boot: a pun on Camillo's usage (line 645) and the footwear Autolycus has from Florizel

686 extempore: unplanned, without preparation

688 clog: impediment, hindrance or surfeit; the word is perhaps suggested by Autolycus' previous play on 'boot'

693 Aside: I will conceal myself
hot: sharp

694 session: court of justice

697 changeling: see Act 3 scene 3 line 118 and note

701 Go to: go on

707 let the law go whistle: let the law try its hardest, it will still fail (proverbial)

711–712 to go about: to attempt

715 I know not: 'not' is omitted in the *Folio* but is almost certainly correct. However if the Clown claims to know exactly how much more his father's blood is now worth this may be funnier. This speech is the beginning of a comic routine, continued in the next act, whereby the incredulous Clown believes that Perdita's marriage will make him a blood relative of the king.

> • *Autolycus describes his place in a disordered world. What has brought about the chaos in which Autolycus' wolfish ways may seem to prosper? Who has it in their power to restore order?*

senses. I see this is the time that the unjust man
doth thrive. What an exchange had this been
without boot! What a boot is here, with this
exchange! Sure the gods do this year connive   685
at us, and we may do any thing extempore. The
prince himself is about a piece of iniquity (stealing
away from his father with his clog at his heels). If I
thought it were a piece of honesty to acquaint the
king withal, I would not do 't: I hold it the more 690
knavery to conceal it; and therein am I constant to
my profession.

Enter CLOWN *and* OLD SHEPHERD *carrying a box
and a bundle*

Aside, aside; here is more matter for a hot
brain: every lane's end, every shop, church, session,
hanging, yields a careful man work.   695

CLOWN   See, see; what a man you are now! There is no
other way but to tell the king she's a changeling,
and none of your flesh and blood.

SHEPHERD   Nay, but hear me.

CLOWN   Nay, but hear me.   700

SHEPHERD   Go to, then.

CLOWN   She being none of your flesh and blood, your flesh
and blood has not offended the king; and
so your flesh and blood is not to be punished by
him. Show those things you found about her   705
(those secret things, all but what she has with her).
This being done, let the law go whistle: I warrant
you.

SHEPHERD   I will tell the king all, every word, yea, and
his son's pranks too; who, I may say, is no   710
honest man, neither to his father nor to me, to go
about to make me the king's brother-in-law.

CLOWN   Indeed, brother-in-law was the farthest off you could
have been to him and then your blood had been the
dearer by I know not how much an ounce.   715

Autolycus, overhearing the Clown's plan and wishing to help his former master, Florizel (whose clothes he is now wearing), intercepts the rustics. He adopts the air of a courtier.

717 **fardel**: bundle
720 **my master**: that is, Florizel
724 **excrement**: literally, 'that which grows out', hence the stage direction, which is not in the *Folio*
727 **condition**: nature, contents
729 **having**: wealth and property
730 **discover**: reveal
736 **give us the lie**: the stress here is on 'give', since the soldiers have bought the lie (i.e. poor goods) with their stamped coin, not been given it
738 **taken yourself...manner**: caught yourself in the act; presumably referring to Autolycus' correction of himself in the previous speech
741 **enfoldings**: clothes
742 **gait**: walk
    measure: stately movement, rhythm
743–744 **Reflect I...court-contempt**: do you not see in my behaviour the contempt of a courtier towards those of low birth
744–746 **Think'st thou...business**: do you think that because I am subtle and tease your business from you
747 **cap-à-pie**: from top to toe

• *Autolycus' pretence of courtly behaviour reflects Leontes' contempt for 'common blocks' and the 'lower messes'.*

AUTOLYCUS	[*Aside*] Very wisely, puppies!
SHEPHERD	Well, let us to the king: there is that in this fardel will make him scratch his beard.
AUTOLYCUS	[*Aside*] I know not what impediment this complaint may be to the flight of my master. 720
CLOWN	Pray heartily he be at ' palace.
AUTOLYCUS	[*Aside*] Though I am not naturally honest, I am so sometimes by chance: let me pocket up my pedlar's excrement. [*Takes off his false beard*] How now, rustics! Whither are you bound? 725
SHEPHERD	To th' palace, and it like your worship.
AUTOLYCUS	Your affairs there, what, with whom, the condition of that fardel, the place of your dwelling, your names, your ages, of what having, breeding, and any thing that is fitting to be known, discover! 730
CLOWN	We are but plain fellows, sir.
AUTOLYCUS	A lie; you are rough and hairy. Let me have no lying; it becomes none but tradesmen, and they often give us soldiers the lie; but we pay them for it with stamped coin, not stabbing steel; 735 therefore they do not give us the lie.
CLOWN	Your worship had like to have given us one, if you had not taken yourself with the manner.
SHEPHERD	Are you a courtier, and 't like you, sir?
AUTOLYCUS	Whether it like me or no, I am a courtier. Seest 740 thou not the air of the court in these enfoldings? Hath not my gait in it the measure of the court? Receives not thy nose court-odour from me? Reflect I not on thy baseness, court-contempt? Think'st thou, for that I insinuate, or toaze from thee 745 thy business, I am therefore no courtier? I am courtier *cap-à-pie*; and one that will either push on or pluck back thy business there: whereupon I command thee to open thy affair.
SHEPHERD	My business, sir, is to the king. 750

Autolycus impresses and confuses the Shepherd and his son but they will not open the fardel for him. He tells them that the king has left his palace.

751, 753 advocate: someone to speak on a person's behalf in court: for the Clown it would perhaps have been more usual to attempt to bribe the judge with a gift of poultry than to employ a lawyer

760–761 His garments…handsomely: the clothes fitted Florizel (see above, line 9 and note, and line 644)

763–764 the picking on's teeth: by his use of a toothpick

771 Age…labour: old man, you labour in vain

773–774 gone aboard a new ship: Autolycus is thinking of Florizel. He is beginning to develop the strategy revealed at the end of this act.

774 purge melancholy: rid himself of sadness; void his body of the black bile which causes melancholy

779 in hand-fast: under arrest

783–784 Not he alone…bitter: he is not the only one who will suffer whatever (torture) human mind can make intense and the desire for vengeance make severely painful

AUTOLYCUS	What advocate hast thou to him?
SHEPHERD	I know not, and 't like you.
CLOWN	[*aside to the* OLD SHEPHERD] Advocate's the court-word for a pheasant: say you have none.
SHEPHERD	None, sir; I have no pheasant, cock nor hen. 755
AUTOLYCUS	How blessed are we that are not simple men! Yet nature might have made me as these are; Therefore I will not disdain.
CLOWN	This cannot be but a great courtier.
SHEPHERD	His garments are rich, but he wears them not 760 handsomely.
CLOWN	He seems to be the more noble in being fantastical: a great man, I'll warrant; I know by the picking on's teeth.
AUTOLYCUS	The fardel there? What's i' th' fardel? 765 Wherefore that box?
SHEPHERD	Sir, there lies such secrets in this fardel and box, which none must know but the king; and which he shall know within this hour, if I may come to th'speech of him. 770
AUTOLYCUS	Age, thou hast lost thy labour.
SHEPHERD	Why, sir?
AUTOLYCUS	The king is not at the palace; he is gone aboard a new ship to purge melancholy and air himself: for, if thou bee'st capable of things serious, thou 775 must know the king is full of grief.
SHEPHERD	So 'tis said, sir; about his son, that should have married a shepherd's daughter.
AUTOLYCUS	If that shepherd be not in hand-fast, let him fly: the curses he shall have, the tortures he shall feel, 780 will break the back of man, the heart of monster.
CLOWN	Think you so, sir?
AUTOLYCUS	Not he alone shall suffer what wit can make heavy

In order to place the Shepherd and the Clown more thoroughly in his power, Autolycus teases them with rumours of the horrible tortures they will suffer if Polixenes should capture them. The fearful rustics eagerly accept his offer and give him gold.

784 germane: related
798 and a dram: and a little more
798–799 aqua-vitæ: whisky
800–801 prognostication proclaims: according to the prediction in the almanac
807–808 being something gently considered: having received an appropriate bribe
813 close: make the deal
815 by the nose: unresistingly

- *What does Autolycus intend to do with the Shepherd and the Clown?*

and vengeance bitter; but those that are germane
to him, though removed fifty times, shall all   785
come under the hangman: which, though it be
great pity, yet it is necessary. An old sheep-whistling
rogue, a ram-tender, to offer to have his daughter
come into grace! Some say he shall be stoned; but
that death is too soft for him, say I. Draw our   790
throne into a sheepcote? All deaths are too few,
the sharpest too easy.

CLOWN   Has the old man e'er a son, do you hear, and 't like
you, sir?

AUTOLYCUS   He has a son, who shall be flayed alive, then   795
'nointed over with honey, set on the head of a
wasps' nest, then stand till he be three quarters
and a dram dead; then recovered again with aqua-
vitæ or some other hot infusion; then, raw as he is,
and in the hottest day prognostication   800
proclaims, shall he be set against a brick wall, the
sun looking with a southward eye upon him, where
he is to behold him, with flies blown to death. But
what talk we of these traitorly rascals, whose
miseries are to be smiled at, their offences being   805
so capital? Tell me (for you seem to be honest plain
men) what you have to the king: being something
gently considered, I'll bring you where he is
aboard, tender your persons to his presence,
whisper him in your behalfs; and if it be in man, 810
besides the king, to effect your suits, here is man
shall do it.

CLOWN   He seems to be of great authority: close with
him, give him gold; and though authority be a
stubborn bear, yet he is oft led by the nose with   815
gold: show the inside of your purse to the outside
of his hand, and no more ado. Remember 'stoned',
and 'flayed alive'!

SHEPHERD   And 't please you, sir, to undertake the business for
us, here is that gold I have: I'll make it as much   820

The Shepherd and his son give Autolycus the gold, and promise him as much again when he has brought them to Polixenes and their business is successfully concluded. Finally, Autolycus reveals his plan to take the Shepherd and the Clown not to Polixenes but aboard Florizel's ship where he will let the prince decide what to do with them. He hope for some reward.

821 in pawn: as security, as a pledge that I will pay the other half of the gold
825 the moiety: half
827 case: situation, skin; the Clown plays on both meanings
833 gone: lost
838 look upon the hedge: relieve myself. The vulgarly comic business also permits Autolycus' final, necessary, soliloquy.
845 occasion: opportunity
847 turn back: rebound, turn out
849–850 to shore them: to put them ashore
852–853 I am proof against: I am unconcerned by

> * *This long scene began with Florizel and Perdita playing the roles of pastoral demi-gods and ends with Autolycus urinating on a hedge. These actions may be considered as having both dramatic and symbolic purposes. As we prepare to leave Bohemia, how do we feel about the country?*

	more and leave this young man in pawn till I bring it you.
AUTOLYCUS	After I have done what I promised?
SHEPHERD	Ay, sir.
AUTOLYCUS	Well, give me the moiety. Are you a party in 825 this business.
CLOWN	In some sort, sir: but though my case be a pitiful one, I hope I shall not be flayed out of it.
AUTOLYCUS	O, that's the case of the shepherd's son: hang him, he'll be made an example. 830
CLOWN	Comfort, good comfort! We must to the king and show our strange sights: he must know 'tis none of your daughter nor my sister; we are gone else. Sir, I will give you as much as this old man does when the business is performed, and remain, as 835 he says, your pawn till it be brought you.
AUTOLYCUS	I will trust you. Walk before toward the sea-side; go on the right hand: I will but look upon the hedge and follow you.
CLOWN	We are blest in this man, as I may say, even blest. 840
SHEPHERD	Let's before, as he bids us: he was provided to do us good. [*Exeunt* SHEPHERD *and* CLOWN
AUTOLYCUS	If I had a mind to be honest, I see Fortune would not suffer me: she drops booties in my mouth. I am courted now with a double occasion – gold, 845 and a means to do the prince my master good; which who knows how that may turn back to my advancement? I will bring these two moles, these blind ones, aboard him: if he think it fit to shore them again and that the complaint they 850 have to the king concerns him nothing, let them call me rogue for being so far officious; for I am proof against that title and what shame else belongs to 't. To him will I present them: there may be matter in it. 855 [*Exit*

Keeping track

Scene 1

1 Summarize briefly what Time says about events during the sixteen-year intermission.
2 What is distinctive about Time's diction and verse style?

Scene 2

1 Why does Camillo think that he ought to return to Sicilia?
2 Why does Polixenes want Camillo to stay?
3 What do we learn of the character and actions of Florizel?
4 What do Polixenes and Camillo resolve to do?

Scene 3

1 What does Autolycus say about his recent past in lines 13 and 14?
2 Why does Autolycus not mourn for the loss of his position at court?
3 How has he come to his present state (lines 26–28)?
4 How does Autolycus attempt to trick the Clown out of his money?
5 Autolycus describes the man who 'robbed' him. What does he say (lines 84–99)? Who is he describing?
6 What is amusing about the Clown's reply to Autolycus?

Scene 4

1 What is distinctive about Florizel's clothes at the beginning of the scene? What happens to his costume eventually and how does it cause confusion?
2 Who else is in disguise during the scene?
3 What different roles does Autolycus assume during the scene?
4 For what two reasons does the Old Shepherd criticize Perdita?
5 Why do both Camillo and Polixenes praise Perdita?
6 After Polixenes has left, what does Camillo advise Florizel to do? Why does he give him this advice?
7 What advice does Autolycus give the Old Shepherd and his son? Why?

Characters

Perdita

1 In what ways are Perdita and Hermione alike?
2 In what ways does Perdita lack her mother's sophistication?

Florizel

1 Florizel displays the following attributes. Find evidence for each of them.
   • He is honest.
   • His love is ardent and sensual.
   • He believes that he can overcome all obstacles.
2 What other characteristics does he have? Again find evidence for each that you list.

Autolycus

(see also the CLOSE STUDY activity, below)
Autolycus fulfils the same dramatic function as the Fool in such plays as *Twelfth Night* and *As You Like It* – he provides comedy of a witty and intelligent kind. He also represents an alternative view of society, challenging the pastoral and courtly worlds of the other characters.
   • Summarize what he does and says which shows that he has a different set of values from any other character we have encountered in the play.

Polixenes

(see also the KEY SCENE activity 3, below)
1 What is Polixenes' view of the relationship between Nature and Art (scene 4 lines 88–97)?
2 What are the inconsistencies in his behaviour and argument when he is confronted with his son's relationship with Perdita?
3 In what ways might his behaviour remind you of Leontes?

Camillo

1 What is Camillo's dramatic role in this act?
2 In what ways does his behaviour in Bohemia echo what he did in Sicilia?

The Old Shepherd

In what ways does the Old Shepherd demonstrate a nobility which exceeds that of either Leontes or Polixenes?

Themes

1 *Time*. A common human reaction is to moan about the passing of time but, based on the evidence in this act of the play, what are the positive benefits of being subject to time?

2 At what time of the year is Act 4 set? Why is this significant? The emphasis in this play is increasingly on *regeneration* and *fertility*. How does this act present these ideas?

3 What further examples of *deception* are revealed in this act?

Drama

1 Scene 1

There are many different ways of portraying the character of Time. In a group of three or four, put yourselves in the role of a production team to discuss how you will stage this scene. Then argue your case to the rest of the class. For example:

- How important are the suggestions for costume and props in lines 4 and 16?
- Is Time played by only one person? How old is/are he, she/they?
- Is there music?
- Does Time have to fit in with the period in which you have set the rest of the play?
- Is Time a comic character or to be taken seriously?

2 Work in pairs. One of you is Polixenes, the other is a spy reporting that you have found Florizel cavorting in the woods with a shepherd's daughter. Points to think about:

- What does the spy expect Polixenes' reaction to be?
- What is safe to tell?
- What will please the king?
- How does Polixenes behave?

3 How would you portray Autolycus' character? Brainstorm some ideas about him.

- Think about how he speaks. Will he have more than one accent?
- Consider the styles of modern comedians that you know. Who would be the best one to cast in the role?
- As costume designers invent his costumes.
- Try various ways of doing his first speech.
- How much does he play to the audience? Are they in on his plans and jokes or is he just talking to himself?

4 Scene 4 lines 168–182

Does the Old Shepherd know that this man is in disguise? What is Polixenes really thinking at this moment? Work in a group of four:

- Two people act the parts of Polixenes and the Old Shepherd.
- Two people speak their inner thoughts.
- After each speech the 'inner voice' says what that character is really thinking.

5 Scene 4 line 433

'*I'll have thy beauty scratched with briers...*'

Use FORUM THEATRE (page 263) to explore this moment of high tension, anger and fear.

- Start with Polixenes and Perdita. How near to each other are they at this point? Is Polixenes actually holding or touching her?
- How is Florizel responding?
- Add Camillo, shepherds and others. Is Autolycus watching?
- What is each of the characters thinking at this moment?

Close study

The song in Act 4 scene 3 lines 1–31

Autolycus is the thievish rogue in this world of shepherds and shepherdesses. His songs and his character provide a contrast to the rural idyll.

1 The first line introduces spring. The second line sounds like a refrain. What is it about? How does it complement and contrast with the first line?
2 Suggest some explanations for line 4.
3 According to verse 2, what does Autolycus feel impelled to do in the spring?
4 How do the first two lines of verse 3 contrast with the second two? What attitudes are being expressed here?
5 What do Autolycus' song and the speeches that he makes before line 31 tell us about his view of the world and human nature? How does this contrast with the views offered by Polixenes, the Old Shepherd and Perdita in the first half of scene 4?

Key scene

Act 4 scene 4 lines 351–449

Keying it in

1 Scene 4 lines 1–52

- Find the mythological references in these lines which refer to transformations and deception. How do they prepare us for events later in this scene?
- How do you view the character of Florizel at this moment?
- What is said here about nobility and the appearance of nobility?

2 **Lines 73–108**
 * Perdita greets Camillo and Polixenes with rosemary and rue which symbolize grace, regret and remembrance. Comment on the significance of this.
 * Why is Perdita so adamant that she should not grow gillyvors?

3 Remind yourself of Polixenes' argument about Art and Nature (lines 88–97). Is there a contradiction between his reply to her and his unwillingness to let Perdita and Florizel marry?

The scene itself

4 **Lines 351–373**
 * What does Polixenes say to his son?
 * Do you find anything strange about his conversation? What reasons might Polixenes have for speaking to Florizel in this way?
 * What is the tone and mood of Florizel' s reply?

5 **Lines 373–399**
 * What does Florizel say about Perdita?
 * How would you describe the style of his speech that ends at line 386?

6 **Lines 399–425**
 * Explain why Florizel is so unwilling to tell his father of the love he has for Perdita.
 * How does Polixenes show in what he says that he has stopped playing a role some lines before he actually unmasks?
 * How does the verse style convey the growing irritation of Polixenes?

7 **Lines 425–449**
How does the situation at the end of the scene mirror that in Acts 1 and 2 when Leontes became so irrationally jealous of Hermione? In what ways are the situations different?

Overview

8 What is your emotional response to the situation now? Which characters do you sympathize with and how do you expect the situation to develop?

Writing

1 Autolycus is just the kind of rogue to sell his story to the popular press. Write the story so far from his point of view, remembering that he is not in possession of all the facts and that his motivation will be entirely selfish.

2 Divide Act 4 scene 4 into separate sections. Justify your divisions and explain the differences of content, style and mood between each.
3 Music and dance are introduced for the first time during Act 4. What is their dramatic and emotional effect?

Sicilia. Cleomenes is attempting to persuade Leontes to forget the past and forgive himself. The king refuses: he will continue to mourn Hermione for whose death, as Paulina reminds him, he is responsible. Cleomenes rebukes Paulina.

2–4 no fault...trespass: Cleomenes uses the language of Christian theology in which the soul of the sinner is redeemed from Hell by his sincere repentance demonstrated through good deeds and worship

8 in them: in comparison with them

12 Bred his...True, too true: the *Folio* has '*Bred his hopes out of, true. /PAULINA Too true...*'. Almost all editors amend this to the text as printed here, which works well on stage. However, it should be noted that Paulina plays on the word, using it to describe the perfect, unparalleled Hermione and not merely the justice of Leontes' judgement upon himself. In doing so she could be picking up on a pun already made by Leontes. Stanley Wells' punctuation, '*Bred his hopes out of. True? /PAULINA Too true...*' (Oxford, 1986) may therefore be closest to Shakespeare's intention.

14 Or from...good: or even if you took some good quality from every living woman

19 good now: please

• *There is an abrupt change of mood and tone between the previous scene and this one. How is this change brought about?*

Act five

Scene 1

Enter LEONTES, CLEOMENES, DION *and* PAULINA

CLEOMENES Sir, you have done enough, and have performed
A saint-like sorrow: no fault could you make,
Which you have not redeemed; indeed, paid down
More penitence than done trespass: at the last,
Do as the heavens have done, forget your evil;   5
With them, forgive yourself.

LEONTES   Whilst I remember
Her, and her virtues, I cannot forget
My blemishes in them, and so still think of
The wrong I did myself: which was so much,
That heirless it hath made my kingdom, and   10
Destroyed the sweet'st companion that e'er man
Bred his hopes out of.

PAULINA   True, too true, my lord:
If, one by one, you wedded all the world,
Or from the all that are took something good,
To make a perfect woman, she you killed   15
Would be unparalleled.

LEONTES   I think so. Killed!
She I killed! I did so: but thou strik'st me
Sorely, to say I did: it is as bitter
Upon thy tongue as in my thought. Now, good
   now,
Say so but seldom.

CLEOMENES   Not at all, good lady: 20
You might have spoken a thousand things that
   would
Have done the time more benefit and graced

An argument develops over the desirability of Leontes marrying again. Dion says that the country needs an heir to the throne but Paulina reminds them of the Oracle. Though she does not believe that the lost heir will be found, she counsels against opposing the will of the gods.

26 consider little: you do not consider enough

29 Incertain lookers on: powerless citizens who can only watch events

29–30 What were...well: it would be appropriate to Leontes' saintly behaviour to rejoice that Hermione's soul lives in heaven

31 for royalty's repair: for the good of the royal house – amplified in the next line

35 Respecting: in comparison with

36 Will: are determined to

45 My lord: that my lord – that is, the king

47 The crown will find an heir: as had happened in England with the accession of James I following the childless death of Elizabeth: the following lines serve as a compliment to the monarch

47–49 Great Alexander...the best: Alexander the Great (356–323 BC) died without naming an heir but one biography which Shakespeare could have known says that he left his kingdom 'to the worthiest'. His empire broke up in the ensuing wars.

49 like: likely

51–52 O, that ever...counsel: if only I had always followed your advice

Your kindness better.

PAULINA   You are one of those
Would have him wed again.

DION   If you would not so,
You pity not the state, nor the remembrance   25
Of his most sovereign name; consider little,
What dangers, by his highness' fail of issue,
May drop upon his kingdom, and devour
Incertain lookers on. What were more holy
Than to rejoice the former queen is well?   30
What holier than, for royalty's repair,
For present comfort, and for future good,
To bless the bed of majesty again
With a sweet fellow to 't?

PAULINA   There is none worthy,
Respecting her that's gone. Besides, the gods   35
Will have fulfilled their secret purposes;
For has not the divine Apollo said,
Is 't not the tenor of his Oracle,
That King Leontes shall not have an heir,
Till his lost child be found? Which, that it shall, 40
Is all as monstrous to our human reason
As my Antigonus to break his grave
And come again to me; who, on my life,
Did perish with the infant. 'Tis your counsel
My lord should to the heavens be contrary,   45
Oppose against their wills. [*To* LEONTES] Care not
    for issue;
The crown will find an heir. Great Alexander
Left his to th' worthiest; so his successor
Was like to be the best.

LEONTES   Good Paulina,
Who hast the memory of Hermione,   50
I know, in honour, – O, that ever I
Had squared me to thy counsel! Then, even now,
I might have looked upon my queen's full eyes,

Paulina extracts an oath from Leontes not to marry again
except with her permission.

56-60 No more such...me: there are no wives like her, so I
shall take no new wife: if I married a wife who, though less
perfect than Hermione, I treated better it would make her
heavenly spirit occupy her corpse and haunt me in this
imperfect world with the question 'Why did you do this to
me?'

59 (Were we...soul-vexed: this line has been much amended
and debated but the *Folio* reading is retained since it is
possible for 'appear' to refer both to 'we offenders' and to the
'soul-vexed' Hermione

61 incense: incite

62 I should so: I should do so

63 mark: look at

67-68 Stars, stars...coals: the stars, like all other eyes, will
remain dead to me. The line refers back to line 64 and
depends on a pun: stars/stares.

75 Affront: confront, appear in front of
Good Madam...done: The *Folio* gives all these words to
Cleomenes but the customary amendment is preferred here.

- *'...and on this stage' (line 58): we are reminded, this
time by Leontes, that the stage-play world impinges
upon our own experience. Consider the various
implications of the word 'appear' in line 59.*

Have taken treasure from her lips, –

PAULINA   And left them
More rich for what they yielded.

LEONTES   Thou speak'st truth.   55
No more such wives; therefore, no wife: one worse,
And better used, would make her sainted spirit
Again possess her corpse, and on this stage
(Were we offenders now appear) soul-vexed,
And begin, 'Why to me?'

PAULINA   Had she such power,   60
She had just cause.

LEONTES   She had; and would incense me
To murder her I married.

PAULINA   I should so:
Were I the ghost that walked, I'd bid you mark
Her eye, and tell me for what dull part in 't
You chose her: then I'd shriek, that even your
        ears   65
Should rift to hear me; and the words that followed
Should be 'Remember mine.'

LEONTES   Stars, stars,
And all eyes else, dead coals! Fear thou no wife;
I'll have no wife, Paulina.

PAULINA   Will you swear
Never to marry, but by my free leave?   70

LEONTES   Never, Paulina; so be blest my spirit!

PAULINA   Then, good my lords, bear witness to his oath.

CLEOMENES You tempt him over-much.

PAULINA   Unless another,
As like Hermione as is her picture,
Affront his eye.

CLEOMENES   Good madam, –

PAULINA   I have done.   75

Paulina presses her argument and tells Leontes that he may
only marry again when she chooses for him the living image
of the dead Hermione. A servant announces the unexpected
arrival of Florizel and Perdita. They are not travelling in
state. The servant is struck by the unique beauty of Perdita.
Paulina rebukes the servant for his tacit comparison of
Perdita and Hermione.

76–77 **if you will...will**: if that is what you are determined to
   do, sir, there is nothing to stop you
85 **gives out**: announces
88 **What with him?**: who is with him?
89 **Like to**: in a manner appropriate to
90 **out of circumstance**: lacking pomp and ceremony
91 **framed**: planned
92 **train**: retinue
93 **mean**: poorly equipped
97 **thy grave**: you, now gone to your grave
98 **Sir, you yourself**: these words are addressed to the servant,
   who appears to be a courtier poet

> • *In what ways does Leontes seem to have changed since
>   we saw him in Acts 1, 2 and 3?*

Yet, if my lord will marry, – if you will, sir;
No remedy but you will, – give me the office
To choose you a queen: she shall not be so young
As was your former, but she shall be such
As, walked your first queen's ghost, it should take
    joy   80
To see her in your arms.

LEONTES   My true Paulina,
We shall not marry till thou bid'st us.

PAULINA   That
Shall be when your first queen's again in breath:
Never till then.

Enter a SERVANT

SERVANT   One that gives out himself Prince Florizel,   85
Son of Polixenes, with his princess (she
The fairest I have yet beheld) desires access
To your high presence.

LEONTES   What with him? He comes not
Like to his father's greatness: his approach
(So out of circumstance, and sudden) tells us   90
'Tis not a visitation framed, but forced
By need and accident. What train?

SERVANT   But few,
And those but mean.

LEONTES   His princess, say you, with him?

SERVANT   Ay, the most peerless piece of earth, I think,
That e'er the sun shone bright on.

PAULINA   O Hermione,   95
As every present time doth boast itself
Above a better gone, so must thy grave
Give way to what's seen now! Sir, you yourself
Have said, and writ so; but your writing now
Is colder than that theme: 'She had not been,   100
Nor was not to be equalled'; – thus your verse

Though the servant asks Paulina's pardon, he will not be
deflected from his judgement. As Cleomenes goes to greet
the visitors, Paulina reflects that had Mamillius lived he
would be the same age as Florizel. Leontes is hurt and
silences her as the visitors enter. Leontes notes the similarity
between Florizel and Polixenes.

102 shrewdly ebbed: grievously flowed away; his praises of
  Hermione have come and gone like the tide
107–109 Would she begin...follow: if she began a new
  religious sect she would dampen the enthusiasm of any who
  believed something different; she would only have to ask
  people to follow her to convert them
115 our prince: Mamillius, who was compared with Florizel in
  Act 1 scene 2 lines 164 ff.
122 Unfurnish me of reason: drive me mad
124 print: copy. Compare Act 2 scene 3 line 98 where Paulina's
  speech underlines the irony of Leontes' words here.
127 His very air: his exact appearance and manner

> • *What is Paulina's role within Leontes' court? What*
> *dramatic purposes does she serve?*

Flowed with her beauty once: 'tis shrewdly ebbed,
To say you have seen a better.

SERVANT   Pardon, madam:
The one I have almost forgot, – your pardon, –
The other, when she has obtained your eye,   105
Will have your tongue too. This is a creature,
Would she begin a sect, might quench the zeal
Of all professors else; make proselytes
Of who she but bid follow.

PAULINA   How? Not women?

SERVANT   Women will love her, that she is a woman   110
More worth than any man; men, that she is
The rarest of all women.

LEONTES   Go, Cleomenes;
Yourself, assisted with your honoured friends,
Bring them to our embracement.

              [*Exeunt* CLEOMENES *and others*
                              Still, 'tis strange
He thus should steal upon us.

PAULINA   Had our prince   115
(Jewel of children) seen this hour, he had paired
Well with this lord: there was not full a month
Between their births.

LEONTES   Prithee, no more; cease;
     thou know'st
He dies to me again, when talked of. Sure,
When I shall see this gentleman, thy speeches   120
Will bring me to consider that which may
Unfurnish me of reason. They are come.

Enter FLORIZEL, PERDITA, CLEOMENES *and others*

Your mother was most true to wedlock, prince;
For she did print your royal father off,
Conceiving you. Were I but twenty-one,   125
Your father's image is so hit in you,
His very air, that I should call you brother,

Leontes observes the beauty of Perdita and remembers how he once had a son and a daughter. Florizel pretends that they have come to Sicilia at the bidding of his infirm father. Leontes greets them warmly. Florizel introduces Perdita as a Libyan princess.

135 **Amity**: friendship
   brave: noble
135–137 **whom (Though...him**: though my life is miserable I desire to live so that I might see him again. Though the final 'him' is grammatically redundant, it serves to place the emphasis on Leontes' feelings for Polixenes.
139 **at**: as a
140–142 **but infirmity...ability**: had not illness, the attendant of old age, taken prisoner the strength he hoped to have
145–146 **all the sceptres...living**: all other nations and their present monarchs
148–150 **thy offices...slackness**: your greetings, so exceptionally kind, are reminders of my sloth and carelessness
153 **the dreadful Neptune**: god of the sea and renowned for his capriciousness in raising storms
155 **Th' adventure**: the risk
156 **Smalus**: apparently a fictional name derived, like some other names in the play, from Shakespeare's reading of the Greek biographer Plutarch

- *Again it is the dramatic irony of which the audience becomes most acutely aware. What irony do you find in the situation?*
- *How does Shakespeare demonstrate Florizel's uneasiness by the way that he speaks?*

As I did him, and speak of something wildly
By us performed before. Most dearly welcome!
And your fair princess, – goddess! – O, alas!   130
I lost a couple, that 'twixt heaven and earth
Might thus have stood, begetting wonder, as
You, gracious couple, do: and then I lost –
All mine own folly – the society,
Amity too, of your brave father, whom   135
(Though bearing misery) I desire my life
Once more to look on him.

FLORIZEL   By his command
Have I here touched Sicilia, and from him
Give you all greetings that a king (at friend)
Can send his brother: and, but infirmity   140
(Which waits upon worn times) hath something
    seized
His wished ability, he had himself
The lands and waters 'twixt your throne and his
Measured, to look upon you; whom he loves
(He bade me say so) more than all the sceptres   145
And those that bear them living.

LEONTES   O my brother, –
Good gentleman! – the wrongs I have done thee
    stir
Afresh within me; and these thy offices,
So rarely kind, are as interpreters
Of my behind-hand slackness! Welcome hither,   150
As is the spring to th' earth. And hath he too
Exposed this paragon to th' fearful usage
(At least ungentle) of the dreadful Neptune,
To greet a man not worth her pains, much less
Th' adventure of her person?

FLORIZEL   Good my lord,   155
She came from Libya.

LEONTES   Where the warlike Smalus,

Florizel describes how they have stopped in Sicilia on their journey from Libya to Bohemia. A Lord enters to announce that Polixenes has arrived, requests that Leontes will arrest the disobedient Florizel and sends word that Perdita is a shepherd's daughter.

158–159 from him...her: from him, who proclaimed her his daughter by the tears he shed when they parted

169 climate: reside, stay

170 graceful: full of grace, virtuous

173 issueless: without children

178 will bear no credit: will not be believed

179 nigh: near

181 attach: arrest

182 His dignity and duty: his princely behaviour and duty as a son

186–187 I speak amazedly...message: my confused speech shows my wonder and my extraordinary information

---

- *Leontes echoes previous images of disease in Sicilia. Consider for example Act 1 scene 1 line 39 and scene 2 lines 297 and 384 ff.*

That noble honoured lord, is feared and loved?

FLORIZEL   Most royal sir, from thence; from him, whose
                 daughter
            His tears proclaimed his, parting with her: thence,
            A prosperous south-wind friendly, we have
                 crossed,   160
            To execute the charge my father gave me
            For visiting your highness: my best train
            I have from your Sicilian shores dismissed;
            Who for Bohemia bend, to signify
            Not only my success in Libya, sir,   165
            But my arrival, and my wife's, in safety
            Here, where we are.

LEONTES   The blessed gods
            Purge all infection from our air whilst you
            Do climate here! You have a holy father,
            A graceful gentleman; against whose person   170
            (So sacred as it is) I have done sin,
            For which, the heavens (taking angry note)
            Have left me issueless: and your father's blest
            (As he from heaven merits it) with you,
            Worthy his goodness. What might I have been,   175
            Might I a son and daughter now have looked on,
            Such goodly things as you!

            Enter a LORD

LORD   Most noble sir,
            That which I shall report will bear no credit,
            Were not the proof so nigh. Please you, great sir,
            Bohemia greets you from himself, by me;   180
            Desires you to attach his son, who has –
            His dignity and duty both cast off –
            Fled from his father, from his hopes, and with
            A shepherd's daughter.

LEONTES   Where's Bohemia? speak.

LORD   Here in your city; I now came from him.   185
            I speak amazedly, and it becomes

The Lord reports that Polixenes is approaching Leontes'
court and has met the Shepherd and the Clown who
travelled to Sicilia with Florizel. Florizel realizes that Camillo
has betrayed him to his father. Camillo is interrogating the
rustics. Florizel admits that he and Perdita are not yet
married.

190 seeming: apparent
194 Lay 't so to his charge: believe him to be responsible
199 Forswear: perjure, contradict
201 divers deaths in death: many horrible ways of dying
202 The heaven...us: the gods spy and inform against us
206 The odds...alike: Fortune favours neither prince nor
    shepherd
211–212 you have broken...duty: you have sacrificed the
    approval of your father to whom you were bound by duty
213 worth: rank

• *'The heaven set spies upon us': Perdita is right to suspect
that she is being watched. Who else has spied on whom?*

	My marvel and my message. To your court	
	Whiles he was hast'ning – in the chase, it seems,	
	Of this fair couple – meets he on the way	
	The father of this seeming lady and	190
	Her brother, having both their country quitted	
	With this young prince.	

FLORIZEL   Camillo has betrayed me;
Whose honour and whose honesty till now
Endured all weathers.

LORD   Lay 't so to his charge:
He's with the king your father.

LEONTES   Who? Camillo?   195

LORD   Camillo, sir; I spake with him; who now
Has these poor men in question. Never saw I
Wretches so quake: they kneel, they kiss the earth;
Forswear themselves as often as they speak.
Bohemia stops his ears, and threatens them   200
With divers deaths in death.

PERDITA   O my poor father!
The heaven sets spies upon us, will not have
Our contract celebrated.

LEONTES   You are married?

FLORIZEL We are not, sir, nor are we like to be:
The stars, I see, will kiss the valleys first: 205
The odds for high and low's alike.

LEONTES   My lord.
Is this the daughter of a king?

FLORIZEL   She is,
When once she is my wife.

LEONTES That 'once', I see, by your good father's speed,
Will come on very slowly. I am sorry,   210
Most sorry, you have broken from his liking,
Where you were tied in duty; and as sorry
Your choice is not so rich in worth as beauty,
That you might well enjoy her.

Florizel begs Leontes to speak to Polixenes on his behalf.
The king agrees. Leontes has also noted a similarity between
Perdita and Hermione, though Paulina criticizes him for his
wandering eye. All leave to meet Polixenes.

215–217 Though Fortune...loves: though Fortune is our
enemy and pursues us in the visible form of my father, she
still has not the slightest power to alter our mutual love

218–220 since you owed...advocate: when you were no older
than I am now, remember how you loved, and speak on my
behalf

221 as: as if they were

229 Your honour...desires: provided that your desires have not
compromised your honour; provided you have not slept
together

232 mark what way: see what progress

- *Florizel ironically appeals to Leontes' capacity for love.
  What further irony follows from Leontes and Paulina?*

FLORIZEL   Dear, look up:
    Though Fortune, visible an enemy,   215
    Should chase us, with my father, power no jot
    Hath she to change our loves. Beseech you, sir,
    Remember since you owed no more to time
    Than I do now: with thought of such affections,
    Step forth mine advocate: at your request,   220
    My father will grant precious things as trifles.

LEONTES   Would he do so, I'd beg your precious mistress,
    Which he counts but a trifle.

PAULINA   Sir, my liege,
    Your eye hath too much youth in 't; not a month
    'Fore your queen died, she was more worth such
        gazes   225
    Than what you look on now.

LEONTES   I thought of her,
    Even as these looks I made. [*To* FLORIZEL] But your
        petition
    Is yet unanswered. I will to your father:
    Your honour not o'erthrown by your desires,
    I am friend to them and you: upon which
        errand   230
    I now go toward him; therefore follow me
    And mark what way I make. Come, good my lord.
                          [*Exeunt*

Autolycus and a Gentleman discuss the opening of the fardel and the amazement of Polixenes and Camillo. A second Gentleman arrives and confirms that the Oracle is fulfilled and Leontes' daughter found.

9 a broken delivery: a poor account

10 the king: Polixenes, since we are told that he and Camillo were questioning the Shepherd (Act 5 scene 1 lines 196–201)

11 very notes of admiration: truly signs of wonder

12–13 the cases of their eyes: eye-lids

17 seeing: what he saw

18–19 if th' importance...be: whether joy or sorrow were signified, but it had to be the extreme of one of these

22 Nothing but bonfires: all about celebrations – an example of synecdoche, a figure of speech in which one element is used to represent the whole

---

• *This is not the scene we might have expected, nor is it what Autolycus had planned. How does it fail to fulfil our (and his) expectations?*

Scene 2

Enter AUTOLYCUS *and a* GENTLEMAN

AUTOLYCUS   Beseech you, sir, were you present at this relation?

1ST GENT.   I was by at the opening of the fardel, heard the old
shepherd deliver the manner how he found it:
whereupon, after a little amazedness, we were all
commanded out of the chamber; only this,   5
methought I heard the shepherd say he found the
child.

AUTOLYCUS   I would most gladly know the issue of it.

1ST GENT.   I make a broken delivery of the business; but the
changes I perceived in the king and Camillo   10
were very notes of admiration: they seemed almost,
with staring on one another, to tear the cases of
their eyes: there was speech in their dumbness,
language in their very gesture; they looked as they
had heard of a world ransomed, or one destroyed. 15
A notable passion of wonder appeared in them; but
the wisest beholder, that knew no more but seeing,
could not say if th' importance were joy or sorrow;
but in the extremity of the one it must needs be.

Enter another GENTLEMAN

Here comes a gentleman that haply knows more. 20
The news, Rogero?

2ND GENT.   Nothing but bonfires. The Oracle is fulfilled. The
king's daughter is found. Such a deal of wonder is
broken out within this hour, that ballad-makers
cannot be able to express it.   25

Enter a third GENTLEMAN.

Here comes the Lady Paulina's steward: he can
deliver you more. How goes it now, sir? This news,

A third Gentleman recounts the proofs of Perdita's identity.
He describes the emotional encounter between the two kings
and their children.

29 verity: truth

31–32 pregnant by circumstance: made plain through
circumstantial evidence

36 character: handwriting

38 affection: natural quality

48–49 countenance of such distraction: their bearing towards
each other of such confusion; subject to such violent change
in their features

50 favour: features, appearance

55 clipping: hugging

57 weather-beaten...reigns: old gargoyle; a weathered, carved
water-spout which has survived the reigns/rains of many
kings – and now weeps copiously

58–60 which lames...do it: which makes any report of the
event inadequate and no description may do it justice

> • *The scene is largely a narrative of events we might
> have expected to see. How could the director and the
> actors, especially the third Gentleman, add interest to
> this narrative?*

	which is called true, is so like an old tale that the verity of it is in strong suspicion. Has the king found his heir?

which is called true, is so like an old tale that the
verity of it is in strong suspicion. Has the king
found his heir?   30

3RD GENT.   Most true, if ever truth were pregnant by
circumstance: that which you hear you'll swear you
see, there is such unity in the proofs. The mantle of
Queen Hermione's, her jewel about the neck of it,
the letters of Antigonus found with it,   35
which they know to be his character; the majesty of
the creature in resemblance of the mother; the
affection of nobleness which nature shows above
her breeding, and many other evidences proclaim
her, with all certainty, to be a king's daughter.   40
Did you see the meeting of the two kings?

2ND GENT.   No.

3RD GENT.   Then have you lost a sight which was to be seen,
cannot be spoken of. There might you have beheld
one joy crown another, so and in such manner   45
that it seemed sorrow wept to take leave of them,
for their joy waded in tears. There was casting up of
eyes, holding up of hands, with countenance of
such distraction, that they were to be known by
garment, not by favour. Our king, being ready   50
to leap out of himself for joy of his found daughter,
as if that joy were now become a loss, cries 'O, thy
mother, thy mother!' then asks Bohemia
forgiveness; then embraces his son-in-law; then
again worries he his daughter with clipping her.   55
Now he thanks the old shepherd, which stands by,
like a weather-bitten conduit of many kings' reigns.
I never heard of such another encounter, which
lames report to follow it, and undoes description to
do it.   60

2ND GENT.   What, pray you, became of Antigonus, that carried
hence the child?

The third Gentleman gives an account of Antigonus' death
and the wreck of his ship, Paulina's mixed emotions, and
Perdita's reaction to news of her mother. We hear of the
recently completed statue of Hermione which is in Paulina's
keeping.

63–64 matter to rehearse: further information to narrate
64 credit: belief
65–66 This avouches: this is sworn to by
75–76 one eye declined...elevated: one eye cast down from
sorrow, the other looking upwards from joy. This is a
proverbial expression and not necessarily intended to be
humorous.
88 attentiveness: her attentive listening to the story
89 dolour: sorrow
90 I would fain say: I am inclined to say
91 Who was most marble: even the least emotional
98 newly performed: recently completed
99 Julio Romano: Giulio Romano (*c.*1492–1546). Shakespeare
may have read Vasari's *Lives* (1568) which quoted Giulio's
epitaph: 'painted statues breathed...by virtue of Giulio'.

> • *The first Gentleman's comment (lines 81–82)*
> *continues the thread of theatrical images which we*
> *have noted throughout the play.*

3RD GENT.	Like an old tale still, which will have matter to rehearse, though credit be asleep and not an ear open. He was torn to pieces with a bear. This 65 avouches the shepherd's son; who has not only his innocence, which seems much, to justify him, but a handkerchief and rings of his that Paulina knows.
1ST GENT.	What became of his bark and his followers?
3RD GENT.	Wrecked the same instant of their master's death, 70 and in the view of the shepherd: so that all the instruments which aided to expose the child were even then lost when it was found. But O, the noble combat that 'twixt joy and sorrow was fought in Paulina! She had one eye declined for the loss 75 of her husband, another elevated that the Oracle was fulfilled. She lifted the princess from the earth, and so locks her in embracing as if she would pin her to her heart, that she might no more be in danger of losing. 80
1ST GENT.	The dignity of this act was worth the audience of kings and princes; for by such was it acted.
3RD GENT.	One of the prettiest touches of all, and that which angled for mine eyes (caught the water though not the fish) was, when at the relation of the 85 queen's death (with the manner how she came to 't bravely confessed and lamented by the king) how attentiveness wounded his daughter: till, from one sign of dolour to another, she did, with an 'Alas,' I would fain say, bleed tears, for I am sure 90 my heart wept blood. Who was most marble, there changed colour; some swooned, all sorrowed: if all the world could have seen 't, the woe had been universal.
1ST GENT.	Are they returned to the court? 95
3RD GENT.	No. The princess hearing of her mother's statue, which is in the keeping of Paulina, – a piece many years in doing and now newly performed by that rare Italian master, Julio Romano, who, had he

The kings and courtiers are gone to see the remarkably lifelike statue of Hermione, so the Gentlemen set out after them. Autolycus realizes that he has missed an opportunity because he was unable to find out the truth during the voyage from Bohemia to Sicilia. The Shepherd and Clown appear, rejoicing that they are now gentlemen.

101–102 would beguile Nature...ape: would cheat Nature of her trade, so perfectly can he copy her

105 greediness of affection: irrational desire

109 removed: isolated

111 piece: add to

112 thence: from that place

113 grace: pleasing quality or event

114–115 unthrifty to our knowledge: waste the opportunity to know more

116 dash: taint

117 preferment: a position at court

124 all one: all the same

126 relished: been acceptable

129–30 blossoms of their fortune: that is, the courtly clothes they now wear

131 moe: more

132 gentlemen born: the title of Gentleman indicated the rank in society directly beneath the nobility and in theory was restricted to those who could trace their gentle birth back through several generations. In practice in Shakespeare's time the title was increasingly used by anyone of wealth and education.

himself eternity and could put breath into his   100
work, would beguile Nature of her custom, so
perfectly he is her ape: he so near to Hermione
hath done Hermione, that they say one would
speak to her and stand in hope of answer. Thither
with all greediness of affection are they gone,   105
and there they intend to sup.

2ND GENT.   I thought she had some great matter there in hand;
for she hath privately twice or thrice a day, every
since the death of Hermione, visited that removed
house. Shall we thither, and with our company   110
piece the rejoicing?

1ST GENT.   Who would be thence that has the benefit of
access? Every wink of an eye, some new grace will
be born: our absence makes us unthrifty to our
knowledge. Let's along.   [*Exeunt* GENTLEMEN 115

AUTOLYCUS   Now, had I not the dash of my former life in
me, would preferment drop on my head. I brought
the old man and his son aboard the prince; told
him I heard them talk of a fardel and I know not
what: but he at that time over fond of the   120
shepherd's daughter (so he then took her to
be), who began to be much sea-sick, and himself
little better, extremity of weather continuing, this
mystery remained undiscovered. But 'tis all one to
me; for had I been the finder out of this secret,   125
it would not have relished among my other
discredits.

Enter OLD SHEPHERD *and* CLOWN *dressed as
gentlemen*

Here, come those I have done good to against my
will, and already appearing in the blossoms of their
fortune.   130

SHEPHERD   Come, boy; I am past moe children, but thy
sons and daughters will be all gentlemen born.

CLOWN   You are well met, sir. You denied to fight with me

The Clown is anxious to prove that he is now a 'gentleman born' and Autolycus is happy to agree if it will avoid a fight and give him the advantage of preferment. The Clown also finds that he can now swear oaths with authority.

137–138 give me the lie: accuse me of lying – a challenge to a gentleman's honour and thus the pretext for a duel

152 preposterous: the Clown means prosperous but the audience will recognize his malapropism as entirely appropriate

159 and: if

163–164 boors and franklins: rustic fools and mere freeholders

164 I'll swear it: further evidence that the Clown is throwing himself into the behaviour which he believes appropriate for a gentleman

---

* *'See you these clothes?' (line 135): the Shepherd and Clown enter in 'disguise' and are having as much trouble coming to terms with their own identities as they have in understanding the identity of everyone else in the play.*

	this other day, because I was no gentleman born.
	See you these clothes? Say you see them not 135
	and think me still no gentleman born: you were
	best say these robes are not gentleman born: give
	me the lie; do; and try whether I am not now a
	gentleman born.
AUTOLYCUS	I know you are now, sir, a gentleman born. 140
CLOWN	Ay, and have been so any time these four hours.
SHEPHERD	And so have I, boy.
CLOWN	So you have: but I was a gentleman born before my
	father; for the king's son took me by the hand, and
	called me brother; and then the two kings 145
	called my father brother; and then the prince, my
	brother, and the princess, my sister, called my father
	father; and so we wept; and there was the first
	gentleman-like tears that ever we shed.
SHEPHERD	We may live, son, to shed many more. 150
CLOWN	Ay; or else 'twere hard luck, being in so
	preposterous estate as we are.
AUTOLYCUS	I humbly beseech you, sir, to pardon me all the
	faults I have committed to your worship, and to give
	me your good report to the prince my master. 155
SHEPHERD	Prithee, son, do; for we must be gentle, now
	we are gentlemen.
CLOWN	Thou wilt amend thy life?
AUTOLYCUS	Ay, and it will your good worship.
CLOWN	Give me thy hand: I will swear to the prince 160
	thou art as honest a true fellow as any is in Bohemia.
SHEPHERD	You may say it, but not swear it.
CLOWN	Not swear it, now I am a gentleman? Let boors and
	franklins say it, I'll swear it.
SHEPHERD	How if it be false, son? 165
CLOWN	If it be ne'er so false, a true gentleman may
	swear it in the behalf of his friend: and I'll swear to

The Clown agrees to swear that Autolycus is valiant and leads him off to see Hermione's statue.

168 a tall fellow of thy hands: skilful and valiant fellow
173 to my power: as far as it is within my abilities
178 picture: representation, her painted statue

> • *Does Autolycus repent? Could you suggest any stage business to accompany the end of scene 2?*

At Paulina's house, Leontes thanks her for all her service to him but, though he has been shown many fine artistic works there, he is impatient to see the statue.

4 paid home: rewarded
 vouchsafed: graciously condescended
5 your, your: an unnecessary repetition; some editors delete or amend believing there to be a transcription error
5–6 contracted Heirs: Florizel and Perdita, heirs to your kingdoms and contracted to marry each other
8 answer: repay
9 We honour...trouble: you take as an honour an event which merely gives you trouble
12 singularities: rarities

the prince thou art a tall fellow of thy hands and
that thou wilt not be drunk; but I know thou art
no tall fellow of thy hands and that thou will be 170
drunk: but I'll swear it and I would thou would'st
be a tall fellow of thy hands.

AUTOLYCUS   I will prove so, sir, to my power.

CLOWN   Ay, by any means prove a tall fellow: if I do not
wonder how thou dar'st venture to be drunk, 175
not being a tall fellow, trust me not. Hark! the
kings and the princes, our kindred, are going to
see the queen's picture. Come, follow us: we'll be
thy good masters.   [*Exeunt*

Scene 3

Enter LEONTES, POLIXENES, FLORIZEL, PERDITA,
CAMILLO, PAULINA, LORDS, *and* ATTENDANTS

LEONTES   O grave and good Paulina, the great comfort
That I have had of thee!

PAULINA   What, sovereign sir,
I did not well, I meant well. All my services
You have paid home: but that you have vouchsafed,
With your crowned brother and these your
       contracted   5
Heirs of your kingdoms, my poor house to visit,
It is a surplus of your grace, which never
My life may last to answer.

LEONTES   O Paulina,
We honour you with trouble. But we came
To see the statue of our queen: your gallery 10
Have we passed through, not without much
       content
In many singularities; but we saw not
That which my daughter came to look upon,
The statue of her mother.

Paulina reveals the statue. It is utterly lifelike, showing
Hermione aged by sixteen years. The audience is amazed.
Leontes and Perdita find it magical.

18 **Lonely**: alone, separate. The *Folio* prints 'lovely' which most
   editors amend but, since there are comparable adjectival uses
   of the word, this may have been Shakespeare's intention.
19–20 **the life as...death**: life imitated as closely as sleep imitates
   death
24 **Chide me**: reprove me (for my injustice)
38 **piece**: work of art
41 **admiring**: wondering

> • *In speaking of 'warm life' and the cold statue, Leontes
>   reminds us of the symbolic disharmony which has
>   dominated the play and may now find resolution.*

PAULINA   As she lived peerless,
        So her dead likeness, I do well believe,   15
        Excels whatever yet you looked upon,
        Or hand of man hath done; therefore I keep it
        Lonely, apart. But here it is: prepare
        To see the life as lively mocked as ever
        Still sleep mocked death. Behold, and say 'tis well.   20
        [PAULINA *draws a curtain, and discovers*
           HERMIONE *standing like a statue*
        I like your silence, it the more shows off
        Your wonder. But yet speak; first you, my liege.
        Comes it not something near?

LEONTES   Her natural posture!
        Chide me, dear stone, that I may say indeed
        Thou art Hermione; or rather, thou art she   25
        In thy not chiding; for she was as tender
        As infancy and grace. But yet, Paulina,
        Hermione was not so much wrinkled, nothing
        So aged as this seems.

POLIXENES   O, not by much.

PAULINA   So much the more our carver's excellence,   30
        Which lets go by some sixteen years and makes her
        As she lived now.

LEONTES   As now she might have done,
        So much to my good comfort as it is
        Now piercing to my soul. O, thus she stood,
        Even with such life of majesty, warm life,   35
        As now it coldly stands, when first I wooed her!
        I am ashamed: does not the stone rebuke me
        For being more stone than it? O royal piece!
        There's magic in thy majesty, which has
        My evils conjured to remembrance, and   40
        From thy admiring daughter took the spirits,
        Standing like stone with thee.

PERDITA   And give me leave,
        And do not say 'tis superstition, that

Perdita kneels before the statue and reaches to touch the hand but Paulina intervenes. Leontes is distraught and inconsolable but will not allow the statue to be hidden. He seems to see Hermione breathe, blood in her veins and her eyes move.

47 but newly fixed: newly painted and not colour-fast

49 too sore laid on: too heavily painted

54–56 Let him that...himself: allow me, the cause of your grief, to take upon myself as much as I can

60 fancy: love and imagination

67 fixure: carving and colouring; fixture

68 As: so that

I kneel, and then implore her blessing. Lady,
Dear queen, that ended when I but began,   45
Give me that hand of yours to kiss.

PAULINA   O patience!
The statue is but newly fixed, the colour's
Not dry.

CAMILLO   My lord, your sorrow was too sore laid on,
Which sixteen winters cannot blow away,   50
So many summers dry: scarce any joy
Did ever so long live; no sorrow
But killed itself much sooner.

POLIXENES   Dear my brother,
Let him that was the cause of this have power
To take off so much grief from you as he   55
Will piece up in himself.

PAULINA   Indeed, my lord,
If I had thought the sight of my poor image
Would thus have wrought you – for the stone is
     mine –
I'd not have showed it.

LEONTES   Do not draw the curtain.

PAULINA   No longer shall you gaze on 't, lest your fancy   60
May think anon it moves.

LEONTES   Let be, let be!
Would I were dead, but that methinks already –
What was he that did make it? – See, my lord,
Would you not deem it breathed? and that those
     veins
Did verily bear blood?

POLIXENES   Masterly done: 65
The very life seems warm upon her lip.

LEONTES   The fixure of her eye has motion in 't,
As we are mocked with art.

PAULINA   I'll draw the curtain:
My lord's almost so far transported that

Paulina tantalizes Leontes further; she stops him from
kissing Hermione but then offers to make the statue move
provided that he has faith and does not ascribe her powers to
black magic.

72 settled senses of: rational mind in
77 cordial comfort: medicine for the heart
86 presently: immediately
91 wicked powers: black magic
96 Or: the *Folio* prints 'On' but this is almost certainly a
misreading of the manuscript

> • *The drama of these final pages is largely visual: the
> language is a simple, direct expression of emotion.*

	He'll think anon it lives.	
LEONTES	O sweet Paulina,	70
	Make me to think so twenty years together!	
	No settled senses of the world can match	
	The pleasure of that madness. Let 't alone.	
PAULINA	I am sorry, sir, I have thus far stirred you: but	
	I could afflict you farther.	
LEONTES	Do, Paulina;	75
	For this affliction has a taste as sweet	
	As any cordial comfort. Still methinks	
	There is an air comes from her. What fine chisel	
	Could ever yet cut breath! Let no man mock me,	
	For I will kiss her.	
PAULINA	Good my lord, forbear:	80
	The ruddiness upon her lip is wet;	
	You'll mar it if you kiss it, stain your own	
	With oily painting. Shall I draw the curtain?	
LEONTES	No: not these twenty years.	
PERDITA	So long could I	
	Stand by, a looker on.	
PAULINA	Either forbear,	85
	Quit presently the chapel, or resolve you	
	For more amazement. If you can behold it,	
	I'll make the statue move indeed; descend,	
	And take you by the hand: but then you'll think	
	(Which I protest against) I am assisted	90
	By wicked powers.	
LEONTES	What you can make her do,	
	I am content to look on: what to speak,	
	I am content to hear; for 'tis as easy	
	To make her speak as move.	
PAULINA	It is required	
	You do awake your faith. Then all stand still:	95
	Or – those that think it is unlawful business	
	I am about, let them depart.	

Paulina commands music and Hermione moves, stepping
from her plinth to take Leontes' hand and to embrace him.
Perdita kneels for her mother's blessing and Hermione
speaks.

98   **Music, awake her**: music, symbolic of harmony, is often
     used by Shakespeare as a dramatic metaphor for the recovery
     of mental or physical health and of social order

100 **upon**: on

106–107 **for then...double**: since (if you shun her now) you
         will kill her a second time

> • *'O, she's warm' (line 109): the simplicity of this phrase,
>   at the heart of a scene in which simple, natural
>   language has predominated, is also the summation of
>   much imagery of hot and cold, life and death, passion
>   and reason running throughout the play. Compare for
>   example Leontes' 'Too hot, too hot!' (Act 1 scene 2 line
>   108) and the playful argument between Florizel and
>   Perdita (Act 4 scene 4 lines 129–132).*

LEONTES   Proceed:
         No foot shall stir.

PAULINA   Music, awake her; strike!   [*Music*
         'Tis time; descend; be stone no more; approach;
         Strike all that look upon with marvel. Come!   100
         I'll fill your grave up: stir, nay, come away.
         Bequeath to death your numbness; for from him
         Dear life redeems you. You perceive she stirs:

                          [HERMIONE *comes down*

         Start not; her actions shall be holy as
         You hear my spell is lawful. [*To* LEONTES] Do not
            shun her   105
         Until you see her die again; for then
         You kill her double. Nay, present your hand:
         When she was young you wooed her; now, in age,
         Is she become the suitor?

LEONTES   O, she's warm!
         If this be magic, let it be an art   110
         Lawful as eating.

POLIXENES   She embraces him!

CAMILLO She hangs about his neck!
         If she pertain to life, let her speak too!

POLIXENES Ay, and make it manifest where she has lived,
         Or how stolen from the dead!

PAULINA   That she is living,   115
         Were it but told you, should be hooted at
         Like an old tale: but it appears she lives,
         Though yet she speak not. Mark a little while.
         [*To* PERDITA] Please you to interpose, fair madam,
            kneel
         And pray your mother's blessing. [*To* HERMIONE]
            Turn, good lady,   120
         Our Perdita is found.

HERMIONE   You gods, look down,
         And from your sacred vials pour your graces

Hermione reveals that she has preserved herself to see the Oracle fulfilled. Paulina has brought everything to a happy conclusion though her own husband is dead. Leontes pairs her off with Camillo and reconciles Hermione with Polixenes.

126 Knowing by Paulina: Hermione herself heard the Oracle (Act 3 scene 2)

129–130 Lest they...relation: unless they desire, at this moment of stress, to disturb your happiness with accounts of their own fortitude

132 Partake to: share with
turtle: turtle-dove – a symbol of faithful love since the bird proverbially paired for life

135 till I am lost: until I die

136–138 Thou shouldst...vows: Leontes refers to his oath to Paulina in Act 5 scene 1 lines 69–72 as well as to his marriage vows

144–145 whose worth...noted: given Camillo's service to both kings, these words surely refer to him (though some critics disagree). 'Richly' is a transferred epithet since it describes Camillo's worth and not Leontes' noting of it.

145 justified: affirmed

147 my brother: that is, Polixenes

149 This: this is (Florizel)

151 troth-plight: engaged to be married

Upon my daughter's head! Tell me, mine own,
Where hast thou been preserved? Where lived? How
    found
Thy father's court? For thou shalt hear that I,   125
Knowing by Paulina that the Oracle
Gave hope thou wast in being, have preserved
Myself to see the issue.

ULINA   There's time enough for that;
Lest they desire (upon this push) to trouble
Your joys with like relation. Go together,   130
You precious winners all; your exultation
Partake to every one. I, an old turtle,
Will wing me to some withered bough, and there
My mate (that's never to be found again)
Lament, till I am lost.

EONTES   O, peace, Paulina!   135
Thou shouldst a husband take by my consent,
As I by thine a wife: this is a match,
And made between 's by vows. Thou hast found
    mine;
But how, is to be questioned; for I saw her,
As I thought, dead; and have in vain said many   140
A prayer upon her grave. I'll not seek far –
For him, I partly know his mind – to find thee
An honourable husband. Come, Camillo,
And take her by the hand; whose worth and
    honesty
Is richly noted; and here justified   145
By us, a pair of kings. Let's from this place.
[*To* HERMIONE] What! Look upon my brother: both
    your pardons,
That e'er I put between your holy looks
My ill suspicion. This your son-in-law,
And son unto the king, whom, heavens
    directing,   150
Is troth-plight to your daughter. Good Paulina,
Lead us from hence, where we may leisurely

All leave to share their knowledge of the last sixteen years.

153–154 **answer to his...time**: give an account of the role he o
she has taken in the intervening years
155 **dissevered**: parted, disunited

Each one demand, and answer to his part
Performed in this wide gap of time, since first
We were dissevered. Hastily lead away. [*Exeunt* 155

Keeping track

Scene 1

1 What is Cleomenes trying to persuade Leontes to do?
2 What does Paulina make Leontes agree to do?
3 How is Perdita described by the servant?
4 When Leontes meets Perdita and Florizel, what is his reaction?
5 What is Florizel's explanation of the identity of Perdita?
6 What news does the Lord bring after Leontes has greeted Florizel and Perdita?
7 What conclusion does Florizel jump to on hearing this?
8 What advice does Leontes give Florizel?
9 What does Leontes feel about Perdita towards the end of the scene?
10 In the final speech of the scene, what does Leontes decide to do?

Scene 2

1 Autolycus and the Gentlemen have just come from the palace. In the first 115 lines they explain what they have just witnessed.
   • What was the proof of Perdita's identity?
   • How did Leontes respond to Perdita?
   • What is the reaction of Leontes and Camillo to each other?
   • What has Julio Romano recently completed?
   • Have the words of the Oracle now come true?
2 What is the Clown rejoicing about?
3 What is his attitude towards others now?
4 What does Autolycus want the Shepherd and the Clown to do?

Scene 3

1 How do Perdita and Leontes react when they first see the 'statue' of Hermione?
2 What does Paulina say to prevent Perdita and Leontes from touching Hermione?
3 By what means, according to Paulina, is she able to cause the statue to move?
4 Everyone is reconciled. What is to happen to Paulina?

Characters

Leontes

1 What persuades us to accept Leontes' repentance as completely genuine?
2 In what ways has Leontes changed?

Paulina

1 What does Paulina do in order to stage-manage the denouement of the play?
2 How does she personify the conscience of Leontes throughout the sixteen years of his repentance?
3 What different reactions have we had towards her since her appearance in Act 2?
4 How is the audience's sympathy turned towards her in the final scene of the play?

Autolycus

What happens to Autolycus during scene 2? Do you begin to judge him any differently as the play draws to a close?

Themes

1 In this last part of the play a new balance is struck between *honesty* and *deception*. What has been achieved through honesty? What has happened because of deception? What conclusions do you draw about the value of each?
2 The tale is a tale of winter but this act is full of the symbolism of spring. What events and characters represent the new start and rebirth we associate with spring?

Drama

1 Scene 2 lines 1–115
Work in groups of three. Discuss:
 • Why did Shakespeare not present on stage the scene described by the courtiers?
 • Why did he want us to see these events through the eyes of courtiers?
 • How would you stage the scene in order to make it entertaining?
 • What are these courtiers like? How do they speak? Are they affected or sincere?
 • Rehearse the scene and perform your characterizations to the rest of the class.

2 Scene 2 lines 128–179

Work in threes. How much comedy can you invent for the final appearance together of the three clowns? Look particularly at the word-plays in these exchanges and the opportunities for physical and vocal comedy. Rehearse the scene and test out your comic talents on the rest of the class.

3 Scene 3

How do you stage the final scene and the 'resurrection' of the queen? Work in groups of three or four.

- Imagine you are statue-makers working for Paulina. She wants a statue of Hermione with the words 'The good queen, Hermione' written on the plinth. One of your group becomes the statue and the others make her into the 'good queen'. How would a sculptor represent goodness? What does Paulina mean by 'good'?

- When everyone is ready, show your statue to the rest of the class. Decide which statue captures Hermione's particular type of 'goodness' accurately.

- With this 'statue', use FORUM THEATRE (page 263) to explore the moment when Leontes says '*O, she's warm!*' (line 109). In a successful production this should be an exhilarating and spine-tingling moment. See if you can achieve this effect.

Close study

Act 5 scene 1 lines 118–137

1 What echoes are there here of things talked about in Act 1 scenes 1 and 2?
2 Which of Leontes' statements are ironic?
3 What do the first five lines show about Leontes' mental state and his understanding of himself?
4 What attributes of kingship are apparent in this speech?
5 The speech has both formal, rhetorical elements and rhythms of ordinary, natural speech. Find examples of each.

Key scene

Act 5 scene 3

This scene in which Hermione is found to be alive is the denouement of the play. All misunderstandings have been removed and we are convinced that everything is ending happily.

Keying it in

1 Perdita is often compared to a goddess. Read again Act 4 scene 4 lines
  1–5, 116–132, Act 5 scene 1 lines 130–133, and 150–155. Remind
  yourself of the myth of Proserpina/Persephone and Ceres/Demeter:
  how might this story relate to Perdita and Hermione?

2 Read Act 4 scene 4 lines 85–97. How does Polixenes justify the value
  of Art?

The scene itself

3 **Lines 18–48**
  The end of the scene will be intrinsically unbelievable. What details in
  this passage prepare us for what is to come by making the statue seem
  realistic and believable?

4 **Lines 49–73**
  * In what ways do other characters attempt to reduce Leontes' sense of
    guilt?
  * How is Leontes kept at a physical distance from the statue and how
    does this increase the dramatic tension of the scene?

5 **Lines 74–97**
  '*It is required*
  You do awake your faith' (lines 94–95). What various meanings could
  these lines have?

6 **Lines 98–121**
  * What is the significance of the music at this point? In what ways does it
    add to the drama of the scene? What kind of music would you use and
    at what point in the scene would you end or alter it?
  * The dramatic impact of this part of the scene is largely as a result of the
    movements of the characters. How do the words act as stage
    directions? If you were directing the play, what further instructions
    would you give to the actors in order to increase the tension?

7 **Lines 121 to end**
  * In the light of the language of grace and divinity used throughout the
    play to describe Hermione and Perdita, comment on the significance of
    the first words said by the queen to her daughter (lines 121–123).
  * Though both Hermione and Leontes want explanations and answers,
    Shakespeare finds ways to avoid these (lines 128, 152–154). Why does
    he do this?
  * What does Leontes do which further emphasizes reconciliation and
    harmony at the end of the play?
  * How does the language used here reflect the return to harmony and
    order?

Overview

8 • Look at lines 15–17, 60–61, 69–70, 85–99. How does Paulina
   gradually lead Leontes to see the statue as a living being and prepare
   him for the reunion with his wife?

   • What relationship can you find between the events, characters and
   language of this scene and the myth of Proserpina?

Writing

1 What factors in the character, experiences and personality of Camillo
  and Paulina suggest that their marriage will prove successful?

2 Write an account of the scene that takes place between Leontes,
  Hermione, Polixenes, Perdita and Florizel after the end of Act 5 scene
  3. (You could write this as if it were a diary entry for one of these
  characters.)

3 Write a dialogue in which Paulina and Hermione prepare for the
  events of scene 3. Try to convey how Hermione would feel about the
  past and her hopes and fears for the events about to happen.

4 What elements in Act 5 are designed to make it dramatically effective?
  How do you react to the drama of the act?

Explorations

A question of approach

When you study a play, you need to be able to see it from two different perspectives simultaneously. You need to be able to imagine and experience the text line by line, sharing the thoughts and feelings of the characters as they go through the events of the play, but at the same time you need to be able to 'look down on' the play as a whole and see the patterns of character and relationship, of language and imagery, of themes and issues.

A play is essentially an audio-visual experience. No two members of the audience see quite the same 'play' and no two performances are ever exactly the same. Two important lessons should be learned from this. The first is that the printed text is not the play; the play is what you see when you go to the theatre. The text is a set of instructions to be interpreted by the director and the actors, artists and technicians. The second lesson is that there is no one 'right answer' to the play, only a range of possible interpretations. Your view can be just as valid as anyone else's, but only if you can present it clearly and support it by valid arguments derived from the text. For this purpose you need, again, to see it as a whole and as a set of details.

Thinking about the play

By the time you have discussed the text carefully you should be beginning to clarify and organize your response to the play as a whole. Most examination questions concentrate on *content* and *form* and these are useful terms which offer you an approach and a framework within which you can prepare to write successfully.

Your first task is to establish clearly in your mind the broad issues raised by the text and the possible areas for discussion, including major characters. You need to consider and discuss some of the possible views and interpretations of these issues and lay down a sensible framework within which personal response can be convincing and well-considered. You also need to get close to the text and identify the key incidents, scenes or even quotations which will form the basis of any essay. When you come to write essays on the whole text, or even a specified passage, the appropriate textual evidence and illustrations should be noted and easily available.

The Winter's Tale inhabits a strange, fantastical world which would seem at first sight to have little to do with our own experience. One way to approach the play therefore is to look more closely at that world and the characters who live there. And if we are to understand these we shall need to know a little more about Shakespeare and his audience.

The court and the country

When we watch drama on television we often recognize clues in the music, settings and style of acting which tell us that the writer is working in a particular genre – situation comedy, the police thriller, or medical drama, for example. Each genre has its own conventions: customs that dictate what sort of characters and situations we would expect. The interest in such entertainment may well be in how an expert writer stretches the conventions.

Literary conventions are nothing new. Shakespeare's audience would have recognized the name of Sicily and the shepherds and shepherdesses of Bohemia and known that he was using a convention called the pastoral. The pastoral is a tradition which began in Classical Greek stories about shepherds (Latin: *pastor*) and shepherdesses who live in a perfect world with none of the cares and complications of the court or the city.

- Remind yourself of what happens during the first part of Act 4 scene 4 (up to the Satyrs' dance). Make a list of all the ways in which the scene is joyful and attractive.

The romantic, rural and humorous elements in this scene are all part of the pastoral convention. Pastoral literature had begun long before Shakespeare. Romantic stories like that of Daphnis and Chloe (Longus, second century) and the pastoral poems of Virgil (70–19 BC) were popular throughout Europe.

However, by the sixteenth and seventeenth centuries the treatment of the genre was increasingly satirical. In *As You Like It* (*c*.1599) Shakespeare uses the flight of the Duke and his court to the Forest of Arden as the basis for a satire both of the morals and manners of the court and of the notion that a rural existence was in some romantic way superior to that of the city. In *The Winter's Tale* he demonstrates similar concerns. Courtly characters shift briefly to the countryside, where the princess has been brought up, but the two worlds are not so very different. Leontes' court is initially, and again at the end of the play, a world of love, though it becomes corrupted; the Bohemian countryside saves and nurtures Perdita but it can be stormy, dangerous and its inhabitants deceptive.

• Under two headings – *Court* and *Country* – briefly list ways in which Shakespeare makes fun of or shows the weakness of each. For example:

Court	*Country*
Leontes abuses his power	Autolycus steals and makes everyone unhappy...

Among other examples you may have noted:

• the flattery of Leontes' courtiers (derided by Paulina)
• the foolishness of the Clown
• the deviousness of many characters
• Autolycus' gesture of contempt in Bohemia when his final act there is to urinate
• Perdita being always anxious about her situation
• the materialism of the Shepherd and his son
• that throughout the sheep-shearing feast its destruction – in the person of Polixenes – is ever present.

The Winter's Tale is played out in the world of pastoral fantasy but this is an uncomfortable story. The 'happy' ending may make us feel uneasy and this uneasiness is exemplified in many of the characters of the play.

• Bohemia and Sicilia each represent various aspects of life in Jacobean England. What do we learn about the society of that time? Can you draw any conclusions about Shakespeare's attitude to the world he lived in? Use the notes you have made as the basis for an answer to this question.

Character

Judging a character can never simply be a case of putting together all the **evidence** of the written word and drawing conclusions. It is more complicated than that.

Characters are revealed by:
- what they say
- how they behave.

Problems

Unfortunately characters are rarely consistent. Major characters, particularly, are subject to change because the events on which the action of the play is based are significant enough to affect the main protagonists: the more important the character, the closer to the action, the greater the reaction. You must always be aware of how characters are developing.

Characters might say or do things for effect: they might be seeking to impress or mislead someone else and not mean what they say at all. Decide if the character is being sincere or if he/she has an ulterior motive.

Characters are also revealed by:
- what others say about them
- how others behave towards them.

Problem

As in life, whether you accept A's opinion of B depends on how you feel about A. If you believe A is untrustworthy or has a perverted sense of values, then A's criticism of B might prove to be a glowing character reference! Alternatively, an opinion might be based on false information, or, again, might be deliberately misleading. It is essential not to accept one character's opinion of another at face value.

Characters are also revealed by:
- soliloquies
- asides.

This may be the best way to assess a character's personality since he/she is sharing his/her thoughts and feelings with the audience. All pretence is dropped because the soliloquy and the aside are ways of 'internalizing' ideas.

Critical moments

At critical moments in the play you can begin to gain better insight into a character by seeking answers to certain questions. There is no formula that will apply to every situation, but these questions can start you off and might lead you to consider other questions of your own:

- What has the character said/done?
- Why has the character said/done this?
- What will happen as a result of this speech/action?
- Could/should this reaction (these reactions) have been avoided?
- What does this incident tell us about the character?
- How does the character change as a result of this incident?

Leontes

We see two snapshots of Leontes' life, with a sixteen-year interval between them, and we are given a little information about what has happened before the curtain rises.

Briefly note the key elements of Leontes' life and character

- in his childhood
- in the first three acts of the play
- in the last act.

Some critics have attempted to use the information you have noted as the basis for a psychological study. They have sought to explain Leontes' irrational jealousy in terms of, for example, his childhood affection for Polixenes.

- Why does Leontes become jealous? Look at Act 1 scene 2 lines 451–457 to help you (but note who it is that says these lines).

The theatrical problem which Leontes' character presents is whether or not he should seem to be jealous from the moment he appears on stage or whether we should see the emotion generate during scene 2.

- Look again at the first 108 lines of Act 1 scene 2 then

summarize the arguments for and against Leontes being jealous from the beginning of the scene.

Hermione

Hermione appears in four scenes and in each the actress is called upon to express strongly differing emotions and to establish markedly different moods.

- In order to gain a clearer view of her, look at Hermione's role in Act 1 scene 2, Act 2 scene 1, Act 3 scene 2 and Act 5 scene 3. Summarize the emotions which Hermione expresses in each, quoting examples from the text to prove your point.
- Look up the word 'grace' in a good dictionary. You will probably find several meanings of the word which you could apply to Hermione. Write them down and illustrate each of them with quotations said by or about her.
- What elements of Hermione's character do you admire? How far do you find her a believable character?

Camillo

Camillo's behaviour is consistent in both Sicilia and Bohemia.
- What is his role in each country?
- What language is used by Leontes and Polixenes to describe him?
- What similarity can you find between the way in which he escapes from Sicilia and that in which he leaves Bohemia?
- What motivates him?

Camillo is seen as a loyal and trusted counsellor by both Leontes and Polixenes. Polixenes speaks of his '*goodness*' (Act 4 scene 2 line 12) and for both kings he is '*priest-like...clerk-like*' – a father-confessor (Act 1 scene 2 lines 237 and 392). At the end of the play (Act 5 scene 3 lines 144–146) his

'*...worth and honesty*
Is richly noted; and here justified
By us, a pair of kings.'
- How far do you agree with this judgement?

Paulina

When Camillo escapes from Sicilia it is Paulina who replaces him as conscience and confidante to Leontes. The marriage of Paulina and Camillo may seem contrived at the end of the play but they are already two aspects of the same persona and, in commanding their wedding, Leontes acknowledges their joint role.

- What are the major aspects of Paulina's character?
- What techniques does she use in order to succeed in a hostile, masculine environment?

Cleomenes rebukes Paulina in Act 5 scene 1 lines 21–23:

'*You might have spoken a thousand things that would*
Have done the time more benefit and graced
Your kindness better.'

- What contrasting qualities in Paulina does Cleomenes recognize?

Autolycus

- Imagine that Autolycus were to be removed from the play. List what you think would be missing in terms of
  a entertainment
  b the story of the play and narrative development
  c our understanding of the world of *The Winter's Tale*.

The wolf in the sheepfold is no mere 'snapper-up of unconsidered trifles' (see Act 4 scene 3 stage direction and note for further explanation). Throughout Act 4 scenes 3 and 4 Autolycus challenges the pastoral idyll, disrupts social and economic order, defies authority and abuses power. Yet we laugh at him. In the hands of an inventive comic actor Autolycus can steal the show. He has numerous opportunities for stage business – comic tricks and mime behind the backs of the other actors – even in Act 5 scene 2 where in some productions he is to be seen picking pockets whilst pretending to be a reformed character.

Polixenes

In Act 1 Polixenes seems to possess kingly qualities which
Leontes lacks.

* Note his major actions in Act 1. What qualities do they
  reveal?
* What do we learn about him from other characters?
* Why might we come to distrust Polixenes?

Polixenes leaves Hermione to her fate in order to save his
own skin. He does so largely at the prompting of Camillo
(who wishes to save himself) but it hardly seems honourable.
In Act 4, when he reappears, his behaviour begs a number of
questions.

* What does he do in Act 4 which seems to be underhand or
  unpleasant?

Perdita and Florizel

* What are the characteristics of the relationship between
  Florizel and Perdita?
* In what ways do their characters differ from each other?

A substantial section of *Pandosto*, Shakespeare's source, is
concerned with Florizel (called Dorastus by Robert Greene)
wooing Perdita (Fawnia). Dorastus 'delighted rather to die
with Mars in the field than to dally with Venus in the
chamber': he is full of princely duty but immune to love until
he meets Fawnia. Shakespeare spares us all the details of his
change of heart. Florizel knows his own mind from the start
though he has little of Dorastus' forethought in anticipating
the consequences of his relationship and planning his escape.
His impetuosity contrasts nicely with Perdita's realism and
resignation.

Old Shepherd and Clown

* What purposes do the characters of the Clown and the Old
  Shepherd serve?

From his first entrance the Old Shepherd offers us a fresh way of seeing events. He may lack the sophistication of the court and its learning but it is he who preserves Perdita and nurtures her to maturity and he who can keep a secret and reveal it at the right time. He is perfectly correct in claiming to be a gentleman born: he has better manners than any of his betters.

• Look at his exit speech in Act 4 scene 4 lines 459–470. Consider not only what he says but the way that he speaks. What does it tell us about his character?

'*What a fool Honesty is, and Trust, his sworn brother...!*' (Act 4 scene 4 line 603) says Autolycus after he has gulled the Clown and everyone else at the sheep-shearing. Although this is not a play in which knavery receives its deserts, Honesty and Truth – however foolish those virtues may seem to be to sophisticates – are abundantly rewarded.

Themes

In the Activity sections at the end of each Act you have been
asked to consider some of the themes which emerge during
the play. In this section we shall look in more detail at two of
these: *Deception and disguise* and *Time*.

Deception and disguise

- All the major characters use deception or disguise,
  sometimes more than once. Copy out the list below, note
  the deceptions and say whether you think their action is
  justifiable. (A couple of entries are made for you.)

	Deception	*Justified?*
Leontes		
Hermione		
Camillo	Says he will kill Polixenes	
Polixenes		
Florizel		
Perdita		
Autolycus		
Shepherd		
Clown	Pretends to be a gentleman	
Paulina		Yes. She brings about the happy ending

- Mamillius and Antigonus deceive no-one. What happens to
  them? What do they achieve?

- Consider the characters and incidents that you have charted.
  What conclusions might you draw about deception and
  disguise in the play?

Many of the major characters appear in disguise, especially in
Act 4 scene 4. Most of the others disguise their intentions and
feelings at some time or another. From a dramatic point of
view this is invaluable: it creates dramatic irony – when the

audience knows more of the situation than some of the characters – and it allows conflict and comedy to develop. But until the very last lines of the play the characters inhabit a world in which things are never quite what they seem to be.

Time

The subtitle of *Pandosto* was 'The Triumph of Time'. Shakespeare's Chorus, Time, says of himself:
'*I that please some, try all: both joy and terror*
Of good and bad, that makes and unfolds error '
(Act 4 scene 1 lines 1–2).
   Add your own examples to the following lists
- Who, through time, is pleased or given joy?
   e.g. Perdita is given joy because, in time, she discovers her mother.
- Who is tested by time?
   e.g. Leontes has to wait sixteen years for his family to be reunited.
- What problems are caused by people acting too hastily?
- What problems are solved by time?

One of the most extraordinary features of the play is the sixteen-year break in the middle. It defies the rules of classical drama and is unique in Shakespeare: in no other play does he so
   '*leave the growth untried*
   Of that wide gap'
(Act 4 scene 1 lines 6–7).
It is, however, an essential part of the plot. The Oracle cannot be fulfilled until Perdita is found, and this depends upon her living to meet and fall in love with Florizel. In the first half of the play Florizel is, like Mamillius, a harmless child; sixteen years later his youthful impetuosity, decisive action and faithful love secure reconciliation for everyone. Time gives Hermione wrinkles but ensures the 'saint-like' Leontes space to pay '*more penitence than...trespass*' (Act 5 scene 1 line 4). There is sufficient time in the play for errors, trials, revelations, joy and the triumph of truth.

It is characteristic of Shakespeare's late plays – *Pericles*, *Cymbeline*, *The Tempest* and *The Winter's Tale* – that, despite the havoc caused by human injustice and the vagaries of Nature, in time order is restored.

- Give examples of the behaviour and qualities of the main characters which make it possible for Time to do its work, e.g. Hermione's patience in waiting until her lost child has been found.

The language of the play

Verse and prose

You will have noticed that Shakespeare uses a variety of different styles within the play. The simplest way of categorizing these is as *blank verse, rhyming verse* and *prose*. (If you are not sure what any of these terms mean, look at the GLOSSARY on pages 269–271.)

- Make a list of those characters who usually speak in prose or rhyming verse and the scenes in which this happens.
- What connections can you find between the scenes where blank verse is not used?

You will notice that the comic characters speak largely in *prose* (though the Old Shepherd uses blank verse at important moments). Prose is also used for narrative reporting in Act 1 scene 1 and Act 5 scene 2. *Rhyming verse* helps to emphasize the symbolic, non-naturalistic, character of Time and is to be found in Autolycus' songs.

Shakespeare's *blank verse* is very flexible. Sometimes it is rhetorical: we feel that the speaker is trying to speak well and impress us with the artistry of his diction.

Act 5 scene 1 lines 24–34

- Read these lines aloud to help you to gain a sense of their rhythm and construction. Try to describe the way that Dion speaks. Look especially at the sound and rhythm of his words and at the structure of the sentences. Does his style of speech tell you anything about his character and purpose?

The first sentence is composed of two long sections which rhythmically balance each other: '*If you would...name; consider little...lookers on*'. Then follow two rhetorical questions which also balance each other – they start with the word '*What*' – and the second is composed of three short phrases beginning with the word '*for*'. Such repetition of a word at the beginning of a phrase is called *anaphora* and is a figure of speech which emphasizes rhythm, euphony (the harmonious sounds of the verse) and consequently the impact of the words. Dion also uses *alliteration* – '*dangers/drop/devour...royalty's repair...bless the bed*' – and in each of these examples the language is being used metaphorically. Dion's rhetoric is appropriate to his courtly character and situation and to the fervour of his argument. His verse is a crafted public statement.

Act 1 scene 2 lines 120–146

• How does the blank verse here contrast with the passage that you have just studied? What does it tell you about Leontes at this moment in the play?

Imagery

Another way of examining Shakespeare's language is to look at the patterns of imagery and their development. For example, one common group of images in the play is related to disease. Camillo develops this image first. In Act 1 scene 1 he says that Mamillius '*physics the subject*' (line 39) but in scene 2, faced with Leontes' accusations, laments his own '*infirmities*' (line 263) and that fear '*oft infects the wisest*' (line 262). He begs the king to '*be cured of this diseased opinion*' (lines 296–297), asks who '*infects*' (line 306) Hermione, and comments on Leontes' '*rebellion with himself*' (line 355). When Polixenes questions him he says:

'*There is a sickness*
Which puts some of us in distemper, but
I cannot name the disease, and it is caught
Of you, that yet are well'

(Act 1 scene 2 lines 384–387).

It is ironic that Camillo, so aware of disease in himself and the state, has been instructed to kill Polixenes by poison.

Camillo is not the only character to use such imagery. Paulina refers to the medicine she brings Leontes and says that her role is to '*purge him of that humour That presses him from sleep*' (Act 2 scene 3 lines 38–39). Camillo has performed the diagnosis and Paulina brings healing.

There are other references to this web of imagery which you may have noted. It is unlikely that, unless we are tuned into such language in advance, we notice the repetition during performance, but it works on a subconscious level to establish a mood and a context for dramatic action.

Themes in the imagery

- Explore the following groups of imagery, listing as many examples of each as you can find and commenting on any ways in which the image changes or develops during the play:

  a horticulture, gardening and farming
  b animals
  c weather and climate.

The play as a theatrical experience

We have looked at the situation of *The Winter's Tale* and its characters in two ways: as a fantastic story, and as a reflection of real life and the way people actually behave. But it is important to remember that it is a piece of drama – artificially designed to capture our attention and manipulate our emotions.

- In what ways is *The Winter's Tale* theatrical? What makes it a dramatic experience? List examples of events and other ingredients.

Among the points you may have made could be these:
- Sharply differentiated characters
- A succession of conflict situations, some potentially tragic, some humorous
- Dramatic irony
- An unexpected ending
- Romantic interest
- A trial scene with a twist at the end
- A storm and a bear
- Comedy
- Song and dance
- A mixture of styles and moods.

The play makes many knowing comments about itself. It is a self-conscious piece of storytelling. For example, when Shakespeare uses a dance from one of the popular masques performed in the royal court (see Act 4 scene 4 lines 344–350 '*dance of twelve Satyrs*' and note), the audience are reminded of it and expected to react appropriately.

Drama activities

If we are to understand the theatrical nature of the play it is worth trying some group drama. At the end of each act there are suggestions for drama activities. Here is an explanation of the techniques. Most of these activities can be done in small groups or by the class as a whole. They work by slowing down the action of the play and helping you focus on a small section of it – so that you can think more deeply about characters, plot and themes.

Hotseating

Hotseating means putting one of the characters 'under the microscope' at a particular point in the play. This is how it works.

1 Begin by choosing a particular character and a particular moment in the play. For example, you might choose Leontes after he hears the news of Mamillius' death.
2 One person (student or teacher) is selected to be the chosen character. That person sits 'in the hotseat', with the rest of the group arranged round in a semi-circle, or a circle.
3 The rest of the group then ask questions about how the character feels, why s/he has acted in that way, and so on. Try to keep the questions going and not to give the person in the hotseat too much time to think.

Variations

- The questioners themselves take on roles. (In the example above they could be Paulina, Hermione, Camillo or Polixenes.)
- Characters can be hotseated at a series of key moments in a scene to see how their opinions and attitudes change.
- The questioners can take different attitudes to the character, for example: aggressive, pleading, disbelieving.

Freeze!

It is very useful to be able to 'stop the action' and concentrate on a single moment in the play. You can do this in a number of ways.

Imagine that someone has taken a photograph of a particular moment, or that – as if it were a film or video – the action has been frozen. Once you have chosen the moment, you can work in a number of different ways.

- Act that part of the scene and then 'Freeze!' – you will probably find it easier if you have a 'director' standing outside the scene to shout 'Freeze!'
- Discuss what the photograph should look like and then arrange yourselves into the photograph.
- One at a time, place yourselves in the photograph; each person 'entering' it must take notice of what is there already.
- Once you have arranged the photograph, take it in turns to come out of it and comment on it, with suggestions for improvements. There are a number of ways in which you can develop your photograph:
  a Each person takes it in turn to speak his/her thoughts at that moment in the scene.
  b The photograph is given a caption.
  c Some members of the group do not take part in the photograph. Instead they provide a soundtrack of speech or sound effects, or both.

Statues/Paintings

Make a statue or a painting like this:
1 Select a moment in the play, or a title from the play (e.g. '*O, she's warm!*' Act 5 scene 3 line 109).
2 Choose one member of the group to be the sculptor/painter. That person then arranges the rest of the group, one at a time, to make the statue or painting. Statues and paintings are different from photographs in two important ways:

- They are made up by an 'artist' and tell us about the artist's view of the person or event.
- If they talk, they tell us about what they can 'see', for example how people react when they see the statue or painting for the first time.

Forum theatre

In FORUM THEATRE, one or two people take on roles and the rest of the group are 'directors'. It works like this.

1 Select a moment in the play (for example, the moment in Act 1 scene 2 lines 175–185 when Leontes watches Polixenes and Hermione walking towards the garden – Mamillius is playing close by and Camillo is apparently not far away).

2 Select a member of the group to be Leontes.

3 Organize your working area so that everyone knows where the other characters are, where characters make entrances and exits, and so on.

4 Begin by asking Leontes to offer his own first thoughts about position, gesture, and movement.

5 The directors then experiment with different ways of presenting that moment. They can:
- ask Leontes to take up a particular position, use a particular gesture, move in a certain way
- ask him to speak in a particular way
- discuss with Leontes how he might move or speak and why – for example to communicate a certain set of thoughts and feelings.

6 The short sequence can be repeated a number of times, until the directors have used up all their ideas about their interpretation.

Preparing for an examination

You will be expected to have a detailed and accurate knowledge of your set texts. You must have read them several times and you need to know the sequence of events and the narrative of a text. The plot summaries in this edition should help you with this. It may seem rather unfair but you will get little credit in the final examination for merely 'telling the story', and simply 'going through' the narrative is seen as particularly worthless in an open-book examination. However, you will be in no position to argue a convincing case or develop a deep understanding unless you have this detailed knowledge.

The questions you may be asked

A-level questions are demanding but they should always be accessible and central, a fair test of your knowledge and understanding. They are rarely obscure or marginal. There is actually a relatively small number of questions which can be asked on any text, even though the ways in which they can be worded are almost infinite. Questions tend to fall into quite straightforward categories or types. For example, you may be asked the following types of question.

Character

You may be asked to discuss your response to a particular character, to consider the function or presentation of a character, or perhaps to compare and contrast characters.

Society

You may be asked to consider the kind of society depicted by the text or perhaps the way in which individuals relate to that society.

Themes

You may be asked to discuss the ideas and underlying issues which are explored by a text, and what are the author's concerns and interests.

Attitudes

You may be asked to consider what views are revealed by the text, what is valued and what is attacked.

Style or technique

You may be asked to look at the methods a writer uses to achieve particular effects. In essence, you are being asked to examine 'how' a text achieves its effects and you need to consider such matters as diction, imagery, tone and structure.

Personal response

You may be asked to give your own view of the text but this must be more than just unsupported assertion. You need to move beyond 'I think...' to a well-considered evaluation based on close reading and textual evidence. It is worth remembering that there is not an infinity of sensible responses to a text.

'Whole text' questions

These questions require you to consider the text as a whole. You need a coherent overview of the text and the ability to select appropriate detail and evidence.

'Specific' passages

These questions require close reading and analysis but sometimes the specific passage has to be related to another passage or perhaps to the whole text.

Writing an essay

Advice from a Chief Examiner for A-level Literature

To write a good essay you need to construct a clear argument based on the evidence of the text. Your essay should have a clear sense of direction and purpose and it is better to start with a simple, coherent attitude than to ramble aimlessly or produce a shapeless answer which never gets into focus. Each paragraph should be a step in a developing argument and should engage in analysis of textual detail which is relevant to the question. You must answer the question set – as opposed to the question you wanted to be set – and you must be prepared to discuss a specific aspect of the text or approach it from a slightly new or unexpected angle. You will need to be selective and choose the material which is appropriate to the actual question. An essay that deals only in sweeping generalizations may be judged to lack detail and substance, while one that gets too involved in minor details may lack direction and a conceptual framework. The ideal balance is achieved when overview and detailed knowledge combine to allow easy movement from the general to the particular, and back again.

Although different examination boards and syllabuses have their own ways of expressing them, there are basically three criteria against which your work will be judged. They are as follows:

- knowledge and understanding
- answering the question relevantly
- written expression.

There is rarely a single 'right' answer to an A-level essay question, but there is not an infinite range of sensible responses to a text, and any interpretation must be clearly based on close reading and supporting evidence.

Ken Elliott

Practice questions

1 Look closely at Act 1 scene 1. What is the purpose of this scene? In what ways does it prepare us for what is to come in the play?
[You should comment in detail on the opinions offered by Camillo and Archidamus about character and the background to the story.]

2 How convincing is Leontes' change of heart at the end of Act 3 scene 2 (from line 140 onwards)? What is the dramatic impact of the last 100 lines of this scene?

3 Read again Act 4 scene 1. Is the use of Time as a Chorus a crude device for surmounting a flaw in the plot, or central to an understanding of the play?

4 Look again at Act 4 scene 4 lines 162 to 350 Stage direction (from the Clown asking for dance music to the end of the Satyrs' dance). What is the dramatic significance of this section of the play? Is there any reason why it should not be cut in performance?

5 Read again Autolycus' soliloquies in Act 4 scene 4 (lines 603–627 and 677–695). What do you find significant in these speeches? What dramatic or other purposes are served by Autolycus in *The Winter's Tale*?

6 Refer to Act 5 scene 3, the final scene of the play. What do you find significant in the language (including the imagery), the symbolism and the events of this scene? How far is it a satisfactory ending to the play?

7 'The Old Shepherd and the Clown are uninteresting characters whose only purpose is to generate simple comedy.' Discuss.

8 'Birth, marriage, decay and death (the cycle of Nature's fertility) are in many ways the structural framework of the play.' Discuss this view of the whole work.

9 'All the important characters of *The Winter's Tale* have been deceitful at some point, with good or bad intent.' Discuss this statement.

10 '*The Winter's Tale* is not so much about the triumph of time as about the triumph of women.' Discuss.

11 'I am a feather for each wind that blows.' Chart the stages of Leontes' passage from happiness to irrational jealousy and back again. Discuss the view that a weakness of the play is the apparent lack of motive for Leontes' behaviour.

12 Through the characters and actions of Polixenes and Leontes we are given various images of kingship. What conclusions do you draw about the characteristics of effective kingship? Is an effective king necessarily a good king?

13 What is the place and purpose of music and dance in *The Winter's Tale*?

14 Does it matter that some elements in *The Winter's Tale* are improbable or unbelievable?

Glossary

Alliteration: A figure of speech in which a number of words close to each other in a piece of writing begin with the same sound:
'But to be paddling palms, and pinching fingers,'
(Act 1 scene 2 line 115, page 15)
Alliteration helps to draw attention to these words.

Anachronism: The writer may accidentally or deliberately make references to things from a later period. For example, the Oracle of Apollo belongs to Classical Greece, while Julio Romano was a sixteenth-century artist.

Antithesis: A figure of speech in which the writer brings two opposite or contrasting ideas up against each other, usually with rhythmical balance:
'FLORIZEL *Mark our contract.*
POLIXENES *Mark your divorce, young sir,'*
(Act 4 scene 4 line 425, page 163)

Apostrophe: When a character suddenly speaks directly to someone or something, who/which may or may not be present. For example, Camillo starts his soliloquy in Act 1 scene 2 line 351, page 31: *'O miserable lady!'*

Blank verse: The main part of the play is written in verse which does not rhyme. Each line has ten syllables which comprise five 'feet', or measures, of two syllables each. The form of the measures, a short (weak) syllable followed by a long (strong) syllable, is known as an iambus. The main form of the language of the play, then, is the iambic pentameter:
'I conjure thee, by all the parts of man'. (Act 1 scene 2 line 400, page 33)
To avoid monotony, this basic form of blank verse is varied by a change in the pattern of weak and strong syllables, and/or by altering the number of syllables in a line.

Dramatic irony: A situation in a play when the audience (and possibly some of the characters) know something that one or more of the characters don't. In a pantomime, for example, young children will often shout to tell the heroine that a dreadful monster is creeping up behind her, unseen. In *The Winter's Tale* we know who Perdita is from the beginning of Act 4 but none of the characters of the play find out until Act 5.

Exeunt: A Latin word meaning 'They go away', used for the departure of characters from a scene.

Exit: A Latin word meaning 'S/he goes away', used for the departure of a character from a scene.

Hyperbole: Deliberate exaggeration, for dramatic effect. Leontes says

> '*Were my wife's liver*
> *Infected, as her life, she would not live*
> *The running of one glass.*'

(Act 1 scene 2 lines 304–306, page 27)

Irony: When someone says one thing and means another, sometimes with the intention to make fun of, tease, or satirize someone else:

> '*Hermione,*
> *How thou lov'st us, show in our brother's welcome;*
> *Let what is dear in Sicily be cheap.*'

(Act 1 scene 2 lines 173–175, page 19)

See also *Dramatic irony*.

Metaphor: A figure of speech in which one person, or thing, or idea is described as if it were another. For example, Hermione says (Act 3 scene 2 lines 71–73, page 93):

> '*Now, for conspiracy,*
> *I know not how it tastes, though it be dished*
> *For me to try how.*'

Oxymoron: A figure of speech in which the writer combines two ideas which are opposites. This frequently has a startling or unusual effect. In his jealous agony Leontes addresses Mamillius as '*sweet villain!*' (Act 1 scene 2 line 136, page 15)

Personification: Referring to a thing or an idea as if it were a person:

> '*O lady Fortune, Stand you auspicious!*'

(Act 4 scene 4 lines 51–52, page 137)

Play on words: see *Pun*.

Prose: In some scenes, characters' speeches are not written in verse but in 'ordinary' sentences – prose. There is often a social reason for the use of prose: it might signify a person/people of the lower classes, or a situation which would not be discussed in polite circles.

Pun: A figure of speech in which the writer uses a word that has more than one meaning. Both meanings of the word are used to make a joke. When Autolycus has stolen the Clown's money he says:
'*Your purse is not hot enough to purchase your spice.*'
(Act 4 scene 3 lines 118–119, page 133)

Rhymed verse: Sometimes Shakespeare uses a pattern of rhymed lines. Often it is just two successive lines (a rhyming couplet) which round off a scene or an incident within a scene; sometimes a rhyme can emphasize a decision or a sense of purpose. Time recounts the events of sixteen years with sixteen rhymed couplets at the beginning of Act 4.

Simile: A comparison between two things which the writer makes clear by using words such as 'like' or 'as':
'*This your sheep-shearing
Is as a meeting of the petty gods,
And you the queen on 't.*'
(Act 4 scene 4 lines 3–5, page 135)

Soliloquy: When a character is alone on stage, or separated from the other characters in some way, and speaks apparently to himself or herself.

Further reading

Two paperback studies introduce a range of approaches to the play. Bill Overton in *The Winter's Tale* (Macmillan, 1989) makes an excellent survey of the work of critics and should stimulate debate. Christopher Hardman's Penguin Critical Study *The Winter's Tale* (Penguin, 1988) is an extended essay which is particularly helpful in describing the literary culture in which Shakespeare and his audience lived. Both books have good bibliographies and will refer the reader on to the standard criticism of the play. Extracts from some of this appear in *Shakespeare: The Winter's Tale* edited by Kenneth Muir in the Casebook series (Macmillan, 1968).

Students will find it helpful to place *The Winter's Tale* in the wider context of Shakespeare's writing. In *Othello* he explores the theme of jealousy to an inexorably tragic conclusion. Other late plays – *Cymbeline*, *Pericles* and especially *The Tempest* – contain similar structural devices and themes to *The Winter's Tale*, and these four plays are often considered as a group, known as the Romances.

The Winter's Tale edited by J. H. P. Pafford in the Arden Shakespeare series (Routledge, 1963) contains the complete text of Greene's *Pandosto*.

Charles Nicholl's *The Reckoning: The Murder of Christopher Marlowe* (Picador, 1992) brings the late-sixteenth-century world of deceit and intrigue vividly to life.